ALSO BY ANTHONY E. WOLF

*"Get out of my life, but first could you drive me and
Cheryl to the mall?" A Parent's Guide to the New Teenager*

"It's not fair, Jeremy Spencer's parents let him stay up all night!"

Anthony E. Wolf, Ph.D.

Farrar, Straus and Giroux

NEW YORK

"It's not fair, Jeremy Spencer's parents let him stay up all night!"

A GUIDE TO THE TOUGHER PARTS OF PARENTING

Copyright © 1995 by Anthony E. Wolf, Ph.D.
All rights reserved
Published simultaneously in Canada by HarperCollins*CanadaLtd*.
Printed in the United States of America
First edition, 1995

LIBRARY OF CONGRESS CATALOGING-IN-PUBLICATION DATA
Wolf, Anthony E.
It's not fair, Jeremy Spencer's parents let him stay up all night
: a guide to the tougher parts of parenting / Anthony E. Wolf.—
1st ed.
        p.   cm.
1. Child rearing. 2. Parenting. 3. Parent and child.   I. Title.
HQ772.W58   1995   649'.1—dc20   94–41604   CIP

*To Margaret, Nick,
and Mary Alice*

Acknowledgments

This book was edited by Patty Bryan. I am deeply indebted to her for her skill and her patience.

I would also like to thank Mike Bryan for his additional editing, Elisabeth Kallick Dyssegaard, my editor at Farrar, Straus and Giroux, for her consistent intelligence and support in this book's creation, and my agent, Joe Spieler, were it not for whom none of my books would exist.

I would like to thank my main three readers, Hugh Conlon, Jane Lamson, and my wife, Mary Alice, who were wonderfully generous with their time to read and listen. I would also like to thank Mary Hurtig, Ann Wolf, Sarah Meiklejohn, Deborah Bergman, and Marsha Liberty, all of whom read versions of this book and aided me with invaluable advice and comments.

Last I would like to thank Martha Cain, Rita Cormier, and Donna Deroche for their help in the production of the various drafts of this manuscript.

Contents

INTRODUCTION   3

PART I

1   NURTURING AND THE BABY SELF

A Potbellied Stove   9
Love Attachment   10
The Move Toward Independence   12
The Baby Self and the Mature Self   13
The Secret Behind Fussing   16
The Baby Self's Other Path   19
Boys and Girls   21
The Mature Self   22
Who Gets the Baby Self?   26
Maturing: How They Become Civilized   29

Contents

    Conscience   **29**
    Empathy   **31**
    Self-Control/Self-Discipline   **32**
  What Good Is the Baby Self?   **34**
  The Problem and What to Do about It   **36**
  The Wonderful Deal   **37**

2 QUESTIONABLE CONTROLS

  Being Reasonable and Listening   **39**
  Trying to Be Fair   **42**
  Power Struggles—The Battle of Wills   **44**
  The Baby Self Inside Parents   **48**
  The Perils of Teaching   **52**
  Rewarding   **56**
  Harsh Punishment   **56**
  Lesser Punishment   **58**

3 WHAT YOU CAN DO

  A Different Kind of Tough   **60**
  How It's Done   **62**
    If You Are Not Up for a Battle   **65**
    You Can Change Your Mind   **67**
    Consistency   **69**
    But What If I'm Wrong?   **70**
  Making Your Decisions Stand   **71**
    Early Controls   **71**
    Parents' Wishes—Parents' Displeasure   **75**
    Guilt   **79**
    Getting Angry   **81**
    Parent Anger and Parent Violence   **83**

Put-Downs—Name-Calling　85
Separation　86
Nagging　87
Business Parent　91
A Secret Weapon: Nonresponse　92
Your Own Self-Restraint　101
Good Listening　101
Survival Training　104
The Ultimate Question　107

PART II　CLASSIC PROBLEMS FOR PARENTS AND CHILDREN

4　DAY IN AND DAY OUT

Whining, Sulking, and Temper Tantrums　111
Whining　111
Sulking　112
Temper Tantrums　116
What Not to Do about Temper Tantrums　117
What to Do about Temper Tantrums　120
When Children Are Angry at Their Parents　121
"I Hate You"　121
"You Don't Love Me"　124
Bedtime　125
Saying Good Night　128
Children in Bed with Parents　129
Getting Up and Out in the Morning　130
"I'll Do It Later"　133
Mealtime　134
Rules for Meals　135

Contents

Picky Eaters   136

Acting Up in Public   138

  Obnoxious at the Mall   138

  Critics of Our Parenting   141

Coming to You with Problems   145

  "Kevin Says He's Going to Beat Me Up"   145

  "I'm Bored"   148

  Grumpy Children   149

5 FAMILY DISPUTES

Fathers and Mothers—Who's in Charge   153

Playing One Parent against the Other   157

Parental Arguments   159

Sibling Fighting   160

  My Sisters and I   161

  What We Did   162

  The Truth about Sibling Fighting   163

  The Rules for Sibling Fighting   164

  It's Their Choice   165

  Sibling Rivalry   166

  Sibling Fighting and the Baby Self   167

  Big Bullies, Little Victims?   169

  If Parents Aren't There: A Witnessed Scene and a Question   174

Divorce   175

  Telling Them   175

  Children Taking Sides   179

  At the Other Parent's   181

  Different Rules, Different Houses   183

  "I Want to Go Live at Dad's"   184

So Well-Behaved at My Ex's   185
Single Parents   186
Lacking a Same-Sex Parent   189
Divorce as a Change of Circumstance   190
Loss of Stability   191
The Long-Term Effect on Relationships   193

6   PROBLEMS THAT MAY NOT BE PROBLEMS

Spoiled Children   195
    Grandparents Who Spoil   196
Lying   197
    "I Want Him to Tell the Truth about What He Did"   201
    Spilled Orange Juice or Lying?   202
    Teaching Honesty   203
    Storytelling   204
Talking Back   206
Getting in the Last Word   207
Aggressive Behavior   208
    Aggressive Play and Fantasy   209
    *What Causes Violence in Children—What Parents
        Can Do*   211
    Competition   213

7   MORE DIFFICULT PROBLEMS

Accepting Too Well   217
Painful Problems in Their Lives   221
Sensitive Children   223
Children Who Worry   225
    Excessive Worriers   226

Contents

Bad Experience in Early Childhood—Trauma   **229**

Difficult Children   **230**

8   THE AWESOME TASK OF PARENTING

CONCLUSION: HAVING A CHILDHOOD   **237**

*"It's not fair,
Jeremy Spencer's
parents
let him stay
up all night!"*

Introduction

Two fictitious—but definitely possible—stories.

1990s—Eight-year-old Jimmy comes into class one morning and his teacher notices the clear imprint of a hand on his face.

"Where did you get those marks, Jimmy?"

"My mom hit me."

Whereupon the teacher, following what is the law in most of the United States today, files a mandatory suspicion-of-child-abuse complaint.

1940s—Eight-year-old Jimmy comes into class one morning and his teacher notices the clear imprint of a hand on his face.

"Where did you get those marks, Jimmy?"

"My mom hit me."

"Well, I bet you deserved it."

Over the last half century there has been a major change in child-raising practice. We now believe that it is not just the lesson but also how the lesson is taught that shapes children. Much that used to be considered normal parenting practice is now viewed as abuse. Hard slaps across the face, repeated hitting, hitting with belts or broom handles, or being locked in a room for extended periods of time are no longer seen as good. Such tactics are recognized as damaging to children— and who they become. Replacing the old, harsher ways is a new child-raising method based on consideration and listening to children. As a result of this change, today's children do not fear their parents as many did in previous generations. And this is good.

But there is a problem with this new way of raising children. If children are not afraid of their parents, they are not as likely to do what their parents tell them to do.

"Lynette, would you please put away your crayons?"

"Why?"

"Because I'm asking you to."

"It's not fair. Kevin never has to pick up his crayons."

Which in the old days would have brought:

"I'll show you what's not fair."

Lynette's mother would have swiftly moved to get the strap. Which is why in the old days Lynette would not even have asked "Why" because she knew why. If she did not do what she was told—and fast—the strap would come out.

But now the strap has all but disappeared. And in the wake of its disappearance an entirely new generation of children has emerged. These children do not talk and act at home with their parents the way children of previous generations did. (As will be discussed in this book, behavior away from home is a different matter.)

"I never would have talked to my parents that way."

Today's children are definitely less well behaved with their parents than their parents were with their own parents. And their parents believe that they have done something wrong. They have failed in some way, because they are clearly not as effective as their parents were. But they fail to take into account that there really has been a change. Their expectations of child behavior are based on what only the threat of harsh punishment can achieve.

They are *not* doing anything wrong. They are doing something right. Only nobody told them what the fruits of their better parenting would look like. Without harsh punishment in the parenting arsenal, child raising is a completely different ballgame.

"Jeremy, would you please move the rabbit cage back into your room?"

"I can't."

"What do you mean, you can't?"

"My arm hurts."

"This is the first I've heard of it."

"Well, it does."

"Jeremy, I am asking you to move the rabbit cage back into your room."

"Why do you always ask me to do stuff?"

"I don't always ask you to do stuff."

"Yes you do. *Always.* You ask me to do stuff and you never ask Melissa to do anything."

"You know that's not true, Jeremy."

"Yes it is. You never ask her to do anything. Only me. You favor her. You really do."

Jeremy starts to get teary-eyed.

Jeremy's mother is beginning to get exasperated.

"Jeremy, I want you to take the rabbit cage back into your room."

"You're yelling at me." Jeremy now bursts into real tears. "You always yell at me."

"I'm not yelling at you."

"Yes you are." Which, at this point, Jeremy's mother of course is. "You hate me."

Jeremy's mother, now very frustrated, grabs Jeremy by the

shoulder intending to repeat her initial request seriously and precisely.

"Ow! Ow! My arm! That's my bad arm! My arm!"

Nobody ever said child raising was easy.

This is a book about child raising that moves into the gap created by the huge but somehow unmarked revolution in child raising that came with the elimination of harsh punishment as accepted child-raising practice. Mainly it is a book about that more difficult part of child raising where we wish to set limits or make demands on our children. And as any parent knows, it is that part that often seems to consume all our time and energy and take much of the fun out of child raising. This book prescribes a method that dramatically shrinks that part to a minimum, thereby freeing you to spend the rest of the time enjoying your children. It is a method that definitely makes child raising easier and more pleasant.

The method emphasizes the power that parents have over their own children because of their child's automatic love attachment to them. Parents traditionally have not learned to use that power. They do not trust their own influence with their child as adequate to produce reasonably (but only reasonably) well-behaved children at home, children who are actually well behaved elsewhere and who very definitely grow into well-behaved and good adults. The methods in this book allow parents to experience that power. The experience can be very gratifying. It can make parents feel that they are very important to their children. Which in turn can make them feel confident that they, and no one else, are the right people for the job.

1

Nurturing and the Baby Self

A Potbellied Stove

The be all and end all of earliest child development is nurturing. It's that simple. Nurturing is the base upon which all else is built. It supplies the core of the personality and the foundation of true self-esteem. I have often pictured this vital nurturing as a little potbellied stove, glowing with warmth, that sits at the center of our psychological being. With it, there is always something to fall back on, a warmth, a feeling-good about oneself. With it, a child will feel comfortable moving out into the world, a child will grow and flourish.

Without that nurturing, there will be an inner emptiness that a child will be stuck forever trying to fill. At the core of that unnurtured personality will be a feeling of "not enough" rather than one of sufficiency. The personality that is then constructed upon this absence, this insufficiency, will rest upon a foundation that is not solid. Without good nurturing, children become much more vulnerable to all the ills and problems that regularly beset humans in the course of a life. Without good nurturing, they constantly hunger to fill an emptiness that does not go away.

A nice thing about children is that they seem to be pretty flexible, pretty adaptable. They seem able to get their nurturing, to grow and to thrive, from many different styles, even different "amounts," of nurturing. D. W. Winnicott, a famous child psychiatrist, spoke of "good-enough mothering," referring to the observed fact that the nurturing that children seem to need in order to develop normally does not have to be totally wonderful, and the amount of nurturing does not have to be 100 percent. Given "enough," they seem to be able to take it from there on their own. Even children who have suffered serious early deprivation do well when they are able to combine their own innate strength with good nurturing given to them later. However, there is no question that there is a bottom line. Below it, children may still come through with no major impairment, but the odds start turning against them.

Fortunately, nurturing is neither complicated nor difficult to give. It is touching, hugging, talking to, paying attention to. It is ongoing loving contact. It is what we as humans do easily and naturally with our children. We love our children. We grab the back of a neck in passing, we give a big hug for no special reason, we lie down next to them and watch television, we have a child who seems too old to sit on our lap do so anyway. This wonderful love, this warm, affectionate, human contact that we all know is the best nurturing in the world.

Love Attachment

Nurturing also builds a primary attachment between parents and children. This attachment is inevitable and automatic, but it is *not* to be confused with bonding. In fact, the concept of mother-child bonding has at times been misunderstood. From the infant's standpoint, there is no such thing as an immediate, powerful, "if you do not have it now forget it" bonding to mother at, shortly after, or even weeks following birth. The idea of bonding as some sort of crucial connection made by child to mother shortly after birth on which the success or failure of their relationship depends is pure myth. Bonding has nothing to do with the psychological development of humans, nor is it the primary attachment I'm talking about.

The crucial primary attachment of nurturing develops gradually and over a period of time. Early in childhood, a child makes a special attachment to a person (or persons) who has been in the role of regular nurturer. This attachment is very special and very powerful. For once the attachment is made, that nurturing person is endowed with great power. It is only he or she who can give this most basic emotional nurturing. Others can nurture a child, but once the attachment is made, only the primary nurturer(s) can provide the special emotional nurturing that is so crucial to a child's developing a healthy sense of itself. The nurturer alone can adequately fuel the little potbellied stove at the core of a child's developing personality.

Fortunately, there is even flexibility in the development of primary attachments. For example, a child orphaned suddenly at one year will suffer following his parents' deaths. But placed in a new nurturing home, most children can make a strong attachment to new parents. Given good early nurturing and continued good nurturing, the special attachment *can* remake itself.

Once the attachment occurs, it is played out: nurturer and child responding and being responded to, loving and being loved—a mutuality of intimacy and sharing. With this early attachment, the nurturer assumes great power over a child's feelings. Parents smile and their baby is in ecstasy, they frown and their child's world is dashed. In their arms, their child is without worry. Parents know everything and can do anything. They keep their children fed, warm, and safe. Should their parents leave, the child frets, wanting them to return. A major theme of this book is that this primary nurturing attachment and the consequent great power that this gives to parents over their children's feelings is the single most important source of leverage in raising one's child. It is where parents find the ultimate power for child control. Parents and child are linked forever.

Indeed, we all know, for better or for worse, how our parents, even when we have left home, gone on and made lives for ourselves, still have a direct line to some place deep at the center of our feelings.

I'm a mature, successful woman. I can't believe how whenever I talk to her, my mother can still so easily get to me.

If you understand the power of this leverage and have confidence in your own influence with your children—especially in the face of all the "I don't cares" and other disobedience you will encounter as a parent in the years to come—you will have a solid foundation for an effective system of child raising.

The Move Toward Independence

As the loving and being loved continue between parent and child, children gradually develop a capacity to nurture themselves, to make themselves feel good. In effect, they become able to pacify themselves when alone. We sometimes describe this as internalizing the "good parent." But, really, it is the internalization of loving and being loved.

Often, young children need some kind of external object to help them, such as a thumb, a special blanky, or a teddy bear. Later they may create imaginary friends. But eventually they are able to hold the whole pacifying process inside themselves. When they are alone, they feel content and comfortable.

When something happens in their lives to make them feel bad (for example, Mommy or Daddy gets mad at them for making a huge mess in the family room), they are able to fall back on something inside themselves to ultimately dissipate the bad feeling. They are not wholly dependent on Mommy and Daddy to make things feel okay. Left on their own, they can handle bad feelings. They mature. They begin to move toward independence.

Normal development pushes toward maturity, independence. Yet there remains a part in children—in all of us—that does not grow up at all.

The Baby Self and the Mature Self

Every day seven-year-old Lance comes home from school, takes off his coat, and drops it on the floor, not three feet from the wall hook where he is supposed to hang it up. He does this every day, and every day he gets yelled at.

"You can't just surprise me one time and hang up your coat when you come home?"

But he never does. Not even once. Lance's classroom at school also has wall hooks for the children's coats. Every day without fail when Lance gets to school he takes off his coat and hangs it on his hook. Every day.

Lance acts one way at home and another way at school. This is the way it is in real life and it's a crucial phenomenon of human psychology for parents to understand. Without it, much of child and adult behavior will never make sense. Like all of us, Lance has two different modes of functioning, which is actually like having two different selves. And in our lives, they operate back and forth like a switching of gears. I call these two selves the baby self and the mature self. At home, Lance's baby self wants what it wants now. It wants only pleasure and absolutely no fuss. Specifically, it likes to unwind and fill up with good stuff after a hard day at school. It likes to relax and feed. For example, it especially likes to sit in front of the television and eat Doritos. But let's take a closer look at the baby self.

The baby self will tolerate no stress. It does not like to be bothered by anything or anybody.

"Lance, just this once will you please hang up your coat when you get home? One simple hand and arm motion. It is not asking a lot."

But Lance never does. When the baby self is in full sway, asking *anything* that it does not *feel* like doing is asking more than it will do.

The baby self cares only about getting what it wants now.

"I promise I will clean up my room all year if you buy me that Megaman Victory Fort."

The baby self makes promises very easily because it recognizes no future. It feels obligated to nothing. The baby self particularly likes the word "later." When used by the baby self, "later" simply gets its parent out of its face for the time being.

It knows no shame and is never sorry.

"Lana, aren't you the least bit ashamed? I caught you red-handed sneaking more lollipops and just after I said you couldn't. Aren't you sorry for what you've done?"

Not the baby self. It's only mad that it got caught.

It does not look at itself and it makes no judgments about itself.

Doesn't Lana care that she has been sneaky and disobedient? No. The baby self does not look at itself and has no sense of itself. It is not good or bad. It is not truthful or dishonest, smart or stupid, pretty or ugly. It just is.

"When I'm home, I'm just me. It doesn't matter what I do. It doesn't matter how I look. Nothing I do counts."

It takes no responsibility for its own actions, nor does it care about the effects of its behavior on others.

"Can't you see how upset your teasing makes your sister?"
"But she was the one who came into my room."

Including parents.

A frustrated seven-year-old Kevin says, "You're the meanest mommy in the world. You are."

Isn't Kevin concerned that this may hurt his mother, whom he genuinely loves? Not at that moment. All the baby self knows is that it is angry at its mother for not giving it its way and it wants to strike back.

And yet later, and when looking back at his miserable behavior toward his mother, when separate from her and switching over to the mature mode, Kevin will feel remorse. And so he returns, as they often do.

"I'm sorry, Mommy. I didn't mean to hurt your feelings. Are you mad at me? I didn't mean it, Mommy. I love you. I don't like to make you feel bad."

And the remorse is genuine. But the next time, when he does not get his way, he will be nasty all over again. For once again the baby self is back in charge.

But, above all, the baby self wants Mommy and Daddy, the main nurturers, and it wants as much of them as much of the time as it can get.

It is this last characteristic of the baby self—its total commitment to feeding on Mommy and Daddy—that is responsible for much of the most frustrating and perplexing of childhood behaviors.

The Secret Behind Fussing

"André, would you please take those two glasses out into the kitchen?"

"They're not my glasses."

"I don't care whose glasses they are. I am asking you to take them into the kitchen."

"I didn't leave them there. Stephen did."

"I said I want you to take those glasses into the kitchen."

"But that's not fair! I didn't leave them there."

"André, I don't care whose glasses they are. I'm telling you to take them out into the kitchen."

"But it's not fair, I always have to do everything. Stephen's a slob and he gets away with everything."

"TAKE OUT THE GLASSES!"

"Don't yell at me, I didn't do anything wrong."

The scene continued downhill from there, ending with eight-year-old André in tears running to his room.

"You always yell at me. You always do. You always do."
And his mother was left feeling furious and helpless.
"You're really asking for it, André."

The glasses remained where they were.

When you think about it, this story makes no sense. Why didn't André simply take the glasses out into the kitchen in the first place and avoid the very unpleasant scene that followed? Why did he seem to create a long, nasty scene *intentionally*, when just a tiny amount of effort on his part would have avoided it? It especially makes no sense given that similar scenes had almost certainly taken place in the past. André knew what the outcome would be when he balked at taking the glasses into the kitchen, yet he provoked a scene that would end with his being genuinely miserable. Why—besides the unfathomable laziness of the baby self, the absolute refusal of the baby self to do any work, to experience any discomfort or stress—did he not simply take the glasses into the kitchen in the first place and "be done with it"?

Parents who have been through such scenes know that often it seems more than just a matter of a child's being indescribably lazy. Their child seems to provoke the fight, and to want it to continue and to escalate. It is as if their child is after something, but it is unclear what. From the parents' standpoint, it often genuinely seems as if their child wanted a smack in the face. Why? What is the child after?

Let me change the previous example. Suppose André's mother made the same request as before, but in this version the rest of the story proceeds a little differently.

"André, would you please take these glasses from the family room out into the kitchen?"

"They're not my glasses."

"I don't care whose glasses they are. I am asking you to take them into the kitchen."

"Oh, all right."

André, perhaps mumbling under his breath, takes the glasses into the kitchen. What happens next? Typically, we would expect that André would go off on his own and do whatever it was he was doing or planning to do prior to his mother's asking him to take the glasses into the kitchen. Perhaps he was going to play with his action figures in his room, or go pester his brother. Over the next half hour, André probably would have engaged in some activity quite separate from his mother.

Now let's return to the first version. In that example, André got the opposite of a half hour of independent activity. What he got instead was a long emotional scene of yelling, scream-ing, crying, and sulking. Rather than time spent separated from his mother, he got a substantial period of time filled with passionate interaction with her. For the baby self in André, this is quality time.

Back in the early reaches of André's childhood, when he was first stubborn about doing something that he did not feel like doing, he made a discovery. He found that fussing could get an emotional response from his mother. He found that if he just kept up the fussing, he could provoke his mother into an ongoing battle, which would continue as long as he kept up his end of it.

> *"You're picking on me. You're always picking on me."*
> *"I'm getting really fed up with you, André."*

André discovered that he *liked* the battles.

On one level, a child may be genuinely upset. André truly believed that he was suffering. Were we to descend suddenly, hook him up to a lie detector, and ask, "Are you doing all this on purpose? Are you enjoying this?" André would angrily sob, "No!" and the lie detector would show that he was telling the truth. Yet on another level the baby self, who was running the show, was definitely having a good time.

Anger is a strong feeling and the baby self, with its lack of boundaries, is just as open to anger as to love. Underneath, André's baby self *was* enjoying itself. Battles, with the give and take of strong emotions, can be quite pleasing and stimulating to the baby self. They become almost like lovers' quarrels. A passionate angry battle is a strong dose of parental contact, and the more passionate the interchange, the better.

The pigginess, the insatiability, of the baby self in its pursuit of parental involvement is beyond description. Let me give a classic example, which will be easily recognizable to all parents.

• • •

Morris and his mother are in a room together. Morris is happily playing by himself, paying absolutely no attention to his mother. But then Morris's sister Sasha quietly comes into the room, her presence unrecognized by her mother. But Morris is well aware of her and immediately drops what he is happily doing and starts demanding something from his mother. As all parents know, the same reaction would occur had Morris's mother gotten a phone call. Morris would have immediately dropped what he was doing to pester his mother for the duration of the phone call.

"Mom, will you help me with this?"

The problem is that the baby self is so piggy that even when it does not want a parent, is interested in something else, has temporarily shifted to the independent mature mode, it is still lurking underneath, constantly vigilant, to make sure that *should* the baby self want its mother, she would be immediately and totally available. And the baby self does mean immediately and totally.

The Baby Self's Other Path

The whole story of the mindlessly piggy baby self can get even more complex. Though its goals never change, the paths that the baby self takes to those ends can be very different indeed. To get what it wants, the baby self will attempt not only frontal assaults, as did André, but insidious, subtle routes as well.

Helena and her mother were shopping for a birthday present for her friend Trish. Helena had found a cute stuffed pink unicorn and a nice leather pen-and-pencil holder, both of which she liked.

"Which should I get for Trish, Mommy?"
"I don't know, dear. I'm sure Trish will like both."
"But which should I get."

"I don't know, dear. I'm sure either will be fine."
"But I don't know which one."
"Just pick one, dear. Trish will like either of them."
"But I don't know which is best. I want you to decide."
"Oh, for goodness sakes, Helena. Just pick one."
"But I don't know which Trish will like. You have to pick for me."

Helena's indecisiveness is nothing more than a passive path the baby self has taken to achieve its goals. Following this path, the baby self takes no chances. Helena invites her mother to take over and merges with her through submission. And unless Helena's mother finally makes the choice, Helena is ready to hold out making a decision forever and possibly to get quite hysterical if further pressure is put on her to decide one way or the other.

What was the big deal? What was so difficult about making such a little decision? If one knows what one wants, there is not a problem. But if one is unsure, there looms the specter of a right or wrong decision, one choice that might have been just slightly better than the other, and therefore the mildest of worries might creep in.

"Maybe Trish really would have liked the pink unicorn better. Maybe she won't like me as much."

The baby self will have none of it because worry equals stress. Where one is not absolutely sure, even the most minute degree of uncertainty creates a situation that the baby self will not tolerate. A rational observer might ask how much stress can be involved in making such a small decision. Not much. But parents have to remember that being rational is not a quality of the baby self.

Boys and Girls

The distinct paths that André and Helena took to similar ends are worth noting because there is no question that, overall, boys do seem to prefer the aggressive path and girls the passive one. The following two statistics make this quite clear.

1. In the United States, four to five times as many preteen boys as girls are referred to professionals for psychological problems.
2. By adolescence, the ratio of boys to girls referred to mental-health professionals is more or less one to one.

If by adolescence, and certainly in adult life, just as many women as men have psychological problems, what were all those future problem girls doing during their childhood years? What were they doing that their problems did not bring them to the attention of their parents or anybody else? *Being good.* If the aim of the baby self is to avoid stress and to get fed, an obvious alternative to combat is to be very, very good.

"I will do exactly what Mommy wants me to do. I will try to make sure that Mommy and I are friends all of the time. I will even try to anticipate what Mommy wants me to do. Her will will be my will. Of course, I will not make any decisions because I could make the wrong one. I will leave all of that to her."

"Is this what I like, Mommy?"
"For goodness sake, Helena, you know what you like."
"No, I don't, Mommy. You do."

They set the table without being asked. They write endless quantities of "I love you, Mommy" notes with hearts and smiley faces.

"What should I do now to help you, Mommy?"

Parents rarely bring their children to mental-health professionals for being too good. Of course, in adolescence—with its mandate that one *must* be independent—the worm turns. And most of the girls who used the passive route as a means of getting a lot of Mommy and Daddy and staying close to them keep the same goal but change tactics. In order to make themselves feel that they are being independent, they switch over to the willful, obnoxious route.

"I'll maintain my sense of independence by disagreeing with everything Mommy and Daddy say. But the disagreeing and arguing will still keep me close to them for lots of feeding, since I'll do it all the time."

With adolescence, boys change too; they usually disappear into their rooms.

Certainly, many boys take the passive route and many girls the more aggressive, but generally it is the other way around. Further, it should go without saying that all children who cling, who write "I love you, Mommy" notes, who fight against making decisions, are not doomed to lives of emotional problems. Their behavior is part of normal development. But one cannot ignore the underlying hand of the baby self where children constantly choose what is most safe. We will see later how this manifestation of the baby self can become quite crippling.

The Mature Self

Fortunately, the baby self has its counterpart, the mature self, that prodded Lance into hanging up his coat at school. The mature self is everything the baby self is not. This mature self does not require immediate gratification. It will tolerate frustration. It can be patient. It has self-control. Unlike the dependent baby self, it is willing to deal with stress in order to work toward a goal. It takes on responsibility, and its concerns are not only with the present but also with the future. Totally unlike the baby self, it is willing to work.

The mature self is self-aware, looks at itself and makes judgments about what it sees. It is pretty or ugly, good or bad, smart or stupid. And as the mature self interacts with and cares about the world around it, not only does it judge itself but it constantly feels judged by others.

"Do they think I am fat?"
"Do they think I acted like a fool?"
"Do they think I am a good parent?"

The independent mature self is just that—independent. It must somehow deal with all feelings on its own. In the most deep and profound way the mature self is ultimately alone and always will be.

Because it knows of the past and future, the mature self can worry. And because it can look at itself and judge itself, the mature self can feel bad about itself—ashamed, guilty, humiliated. Because it is alone, and knows that it is alone, it can feel vulnerable. And because of all the above, the mature self feels responsibility for its own actions, which can be a source of great pride or a terrible burden.

This mature self pursues a second kind of nurturing that is different from the primary nurturing the baby self desires. The mature self turns outward from home and family for its nurturing.

A three-year-old boy is trying to build a block tower. After a number of attempts, he is unable to balance more than two blocks on top of each other. His mother, watching, comes over and, wishing to help, starts to put on a third block. The boy pushes away his mother's hand.

For the mature self, nurturing comes from its sense of competence and acceptance in dealing with the world separate from parents and home. The mature self is the part of the child that explores, that seeks out what is new. The mature self is the part that enjoys and cares about friends. It is the part that wants to look into cupboards and put on its own socks. It is the part that wants to acquire skills, to be good in sports and games, and to do well in school.

Early on, primary nurturing of the baby self is far and away the most important. But as children get older, increasingly their sense of well-being depends on nurturing of the mature self. Less and less can primary nurturing make everything all right. The milk of parental love is simply not as nourishing as it used to be. Past a certain age, "You do look lovely, Sharon" or "Well, Stephen, *we* think you are a wonderful boy" usually brings little more than a shrug or a grimace when once they would have brought a beaming smile.

"Of course they have to say that. They're my parents."

The mature self is charged with the very important job of learning how to survive on one's own. For finally one day the child does go out into the big world. Ultimately, it will even make new primary love attachments—to friends, lovers, spouses, and finally to its own children.

"I do love you, Mom. It's just that Lorraine and the kids have to come first. You know that."

It is what we call maturing. It is what the mature self does.

The baby self and the mature self exist as two wholly separate and complete systems of behavior. Each has its own set of rules, perceptions, and even differing sets of feelings (for example, embarrassment does not exist in the baby-self mode). The only problem is that we so rarely get to see the mature self. For the domain of the baby self is at home and with parents. The good behaviors that we wish to instill in our children do come out—but usually away from us, at other people's houses, at school.

At nursery school, a three-year-old cries and will not play with the other children as long as either of her parents is present. But as soon as they leave, she stops crying and happily joins the other children.

A ten-year-old girl gives her parents nothing but grief at home and would prefer death to helping around the house. Inexplicably, her grandmother reports that on occasional weekend visits her granddaughter is always pleasant and regularly offers help with household chores.

"She did? Are you sure it was our Tracy?"

A teenage girl allows herself to look like a slob when she is at home. But she fusses with her appearance for over an hour to get herself ready for school.

A seven-year-old boy is bossy with his parents and siblings but with everyone else he is very polite, even timid.

We simply get a different version of our child than the rest of the world does.

As parents we see these differences as inconsistent and perplexing.

"How come you never act like that when you're with us?"

But for children it all seems totally natural. If they see themselves as considerate, honest, hard working when they are out in the big world, the fact that they are inconsiderate, dishonest, and lazy when at home is just not a problem. Though intellectually they can appreciate the inconsistency of their behavior, they cannot *feel* it.

"I can't explain it. It's just different when I am at school or somewhere else. I don't know. At home doesn't count."

That's the best they can do to articulate their different behaviors. To children, the unspoken lines between the two domains are an automatic part of their lives. They assume that parents will understand and are simply puzzled when they do not.

But then comes the important question: Which of these two—the at-home version or the one away from home is the better indicator of who our children really are and who they will become as adults? The answer, as time invariably shows, is that it is not the behavior of the baby self but the behavior of the independent, mature self, functioning in its realm away from home, that is the far more accurate reflection of the adult-to-be. But it is the baby self that parents usually get to see, which has huge implications for parenting. For parents are faced with the overwhelming paradox of child raising: What you see is not what you get.

Who Gets the Baby Self?

Where, when, and with whom the baby self chooses to appear is not always easy to understand. Its ability to appear and disappear in different places and with different people can be downright perplexing.

Seven-year-old Luke and his mother were in the family room. Luke, pursuing scientific curiosity, began playing with a lamp that had a variable-watt bulb. He was interested in both the three-way effect and in how quickly or how slowly he could turn the light on and off. Luke's mother was trying to read by that same lamp.

"Luke, please stop that. It's very irritating. I'm trying to read."

Luke, seeming not to hear his mother at all, continued his experiments.

"Luke, did you hear me? I said stop playing with the lamp."

"You can read. It's not bothering you," said Luke, turning the switch many times as if to demonstrate his point.

"Luke, I said stop playing with the lamp!" Luke's mother's voice was now getting louder as she was getting more aggravated.

"You don't have to yell at me. You don't have to yell at me all the time," shouted Luke, who was also now angry and continuing to turn the switch.

At that point, Luke's father, hearing the commotion, entered the room. He strode over to Luke.

"Luke. Stop that. Now."

Luke immediately backed off from the lamp.

"Barbara, you're just not firm enough with Luke," said Luke's father, irritated that he had had to interrupt his paperwork in order to come in and deal with the problem.

Luke's mother, though resentful of her husband's comment, said nothing. She basically felt he was right. This was not the first time that such a scenario had been played out. Clearly, Luke did respond better to his father's interventions than to hers. Luke almost always gave her some kind of flack, but he virtually never gave any to his father. Luke's father never hit him and was not intimidating, yet Luke usually jumped at his father's commands while he usually ignored or fussed at his mother's, no matter what she did.

Though Luke's mother hated to admit it, Luke's father must somehow be doing it right while she obviously was not dealing with Luke properly. This did not make sense to her because she knew that she was generally a tougher person than her husband. Yet from the way that Luke responded to the two of them, it seemed just the opposite.

A second story:

For a number of years, Barbara's and Joseph's work schedules dictated that Joseph was home most of the time when the children were out of school. He was also on duty for bedtime, which was a battle every night because, among other things, his daughter Jennifer would procrastinate endlessly.

"But my show's not over."

And the twins, Derek and Dugan, would fight and fuss endlessly.

"Dad, Derek took my pajamas."

"Dugan spit on mine. My pajamas have spit on them."

Bedtime was always a struggle. Joseph was invariably exhausted by the time the three were finally in bed except on Thursday nights, when Barbara was home and had the honors.

"I'm ready for bed, Mom," called Jennifer punctually at her bedtime. "Come kiss me good night."

"Look how good we are," said the twins, appearing washed, toothbrushed, and neatly pajamaed to present themselves to their mother.

But then the next night, when their father was in charge, bedtime was the usual chaos.

"Why can't you three ever go to bed for me the way you do for your mother?" asked an exasperated Joseph.

"Mommy's nicer," said the twins as they ran into the kitchen for potato chips.

A chief characteristic of the baby self is that it comes out more with the *primary* nurturer in the children's lives. Other adults, who are cared about but who are not primary nurturers, tend to get far more of the mature self who wants self-respect, who wants to feel proud. Children also care that their primary nurturer is proud of them, but they care more that their primary nurturer is there to give love unconditionally. That love they always want to be able to take for granted, even if their behavior is not always something of which they are proud. Unconditional love. Thus Luke presented his mother with his baby self and his father with his mature self. But Barbara and Joseph's children were just the opposite, frustrating their father at bedtime with their baby selves, because he was the primary nurturer in that family.

In today's families, mother-father roles are not fixed. Where fathers are the main parent and mothers are either absent or in a distinctly lesser role, the father will be the primary nurturer. Where fathers have all along been just as involved in the child raising as mothers, *both* can just as easily be in the nurturer role. *The gender of the parent has nothing to do with which "version" of their child they get.* It is their roles in the life of their child that determine that. If you are the primary nurturer, you get more of the baby self. If you are distinctly less present day to day, you tend to see the better behavior of the mature self.

Orlando behaved excellently the whole time he was at his friend Michael's house. But when his mother arrived and started chatting with Michael's mother, Orlando's behavior mysteriously deteriorated. He began whining and fussing.

"I don't understand," said Michael's mother. "He was so good until you came."

Maturing: How They Become Civilized

Conscience

But if the mature self is the part that is in charge of self-control, of doing what the child is supposed to do, of becoming civilized—where does it come from? It does not spring out of nothing. How do children learn to be civilized?

In earliest childhood, when the mature self is just starting out, it has little role in child control. That is the parents' job.

"Don't," says Derek's mother as she grabs his cereal bowl just before he intentionally tips it onto the floor.

But if children become attached to a parent, they automatically not only take in the loving parent and make him or her a nurturing part of themselves, they take in the whole package. Parents' rules included. They cannot help it.

And so they begin to develop a conscience. Initially that conscience is the internalized voice of the parent floating around in their children's heads.

"Mom will get mad if I don't pick up my room."
"Dad will get mad if I don't brush my teeth."
"Mom will yell at me if I come home from Kevin's house after it starts getting dark."

And because of the basic love attachment, this voice has power. Going against this voice, not obeying this voice, causes discomfort and *always* has an accompanying sense of unease.

"I know it's getting dark and I should go home but we're in the middle of a game and I don't want to stop. I'm not gonna. I don't care if Mom gets mad. It's a stupid rule."

But the sense of unease is there. Of course, the pull of the conscience may not always be enough to produce obedience because, in any given instance, the forces working against the conscience may be too strong.

"I'm not gonna go. I'm just having too good a time."

But often the pull, the unease, wins out.

"I gotta go, Kevin, or my mom will have a fit. See ya."

This voice, the conscience, is of course a voice that only the mature self hears. The baby self never hears its call. Therefore, the voice will kick in when the child is apart from the parent, even if it's just in his room.

"I really shouldn't have called Mom a jerk."

But when he said it to her face, baby self in charge, she genuinely seemed to deserve it.

Over time, the voice, the developing conscience, automatically undergoes a transformation. Increasingly, the voice, rather than sounding like a parent's, sounds more and more like one's own voice. "I should clean up my room or else Mom will be mad" becomes "I should clean up my room. It really looks messy."

This gradual transformation is the internalization, the taking in as one's own, of one's parents' wishes and values. It is where our rules for them, our wants for them, get transformed into their own rules and wants for themselves. It is the formation of their own adult conscience.

Empathy

Another major source of control that becomes part of the mature self's conscience is what we call empathy.

Empathy is knowing that others have feelings just as we do, and genuinely taking pain or pleasure in what happens to them. It's the kindest part of the conscience. Children develop empathy not from any learned sense of right or wrong, but from the sense that we, as human beings, genuinely care about others. We suffer or feel pleasure not just from what happens to us, but from what happens to others as well. A child is unable to tease the class bozo because he *knows* how the teasing will make him feel and will feel discomfort at the other's suffering. In the long run, empathy is perhaps the single most important of all behavior controls.

The main requirement for the development of empathy is

good nurturing. Empathy develops from being treated lovingly, caringly, and selflessly. Empathy comes from having been cared about and from having one's own feelings taken into consideration. It comes from having been part of a loving relationship. It's a fact of child development that children who are raised with love and consideration are able to give the same to others.

However, even children who are not raised in loving and caring relationships can develop empathy. Some who are ill-treated as children latch on to an adult who is not a major caregiver in their lives—a teacher, a grandparent, anyone who has been kind to them—and somehow use that small piece of compassion as a foundation for their own caring for others.

Self-Control/Self-Discipline

The last major piece of becoming civilized is the actual ability to control oneself. Along with the development of a con-science, the mature self has to supply the self-discipline to heed that conscience. Without self-discipline, a child may not wish to take the candy that Mom was saving for her bridge club because he thinks it is wrong, but he's just too hungry and he wants the candy too much. So he takes it and eats it anyway. A person can genuinely know what is right, want to do it, mean to do it, but lack the capacity, the self-discipline, the maturity to act as he wishes. I may be the nicest guy in the world, genuinely wanting to do the right thing, but if I am still just a big baby, with little tolerance for frustration, with little ability to deal with not getting my way, I will act badly.

"I really did mean to come to your party, like I said I would, but I met these guys and we got to talking, and anyway, I spent the evening in a bar with them."

"I really didn't want to hurt her, but I just got so mad when she started yelling at me. I just couldn't stop myself."

"I wanted to finish high school. I didn't want to disappoint Mom and Dad, but I never seemed able to get myself to do the work."

That is, it is all well and good to have an excellent empathic conscience, to be in our hearts good people, but we also need the strength to have our actions back up our beliefs.

These are the basic elements of becoming civilized. Internalizing parents' values, genuine caring for others, and the capacity for self-discipline. How do children acquire them? Where do they come from?

The answer is that if parents are doing their job—nurturing, but also, as will be discussed, making demands and setting limits—the mature self will have all it needs to grow, just as it should. It will get bigger, stronger. Its role will increase. And in time the mature self will take on an executive role. It will take charge of deciding the when and the where of the two selves. It decides when we need to act in a mature manner, and when it is okay for us to give the baby self free rein. To the mature self falls the job of keeping the baby self in its appropriate place. Eventually, the mature self actually controls the shifting back and forth between the two modes.

At the office Christmas party, I have to watch what I say and do. But at Harry and Vivian's New Year's Eve party, I can act like a total jerk and nobody is going to care. Not even Lou Anne.

When I come home from the office, there is half an hour when everybody has to leave me alone. When I am just going to veg out. When I do not have to hear about anybody's day. But after that half hour, I am available. I'll make supper and the kids can tell me about anything they want to, and I'll listen.

That control never becomes perfect. But by adulthood, with most of us, it works well enough. That is, we can work when we need to work and we can play and relax when it is time to play and relax.

Baby selves will always act like baby selves. They do not change. But mature selves do. During childhood, the mature self is growing. While the baby self keeps going nowhere, the mature self is getting stronger, taking on ever-increasing responsibility until finally it becomes a full, genuine, adult, mature self.

What Good Is the Baby Self?

A fact of life is that the realm of the mature self is also the realm of stress. Therefore, with children and adults as well, the baby self is our retreat where we can go to relax, unwind, and free ourselves from all the worries and stresses of our everyday lives. It is a time-out place, like a corner in a boxing match between rounds, where we can nurture ourselves, regroup, and head out again into the fray.

It can even be a part of us separate from who we are in the world out there, separate from what we have accomplished, separate from what others think of us. It can be a part of us that just *is*, not good, not bad, not successful, not a failure. It is not the part of me who may or may not get promoted to vice president in charge of sales, not the part who is or is not popular in school, good or not at school work, good or not at sports, but it is the part of me who likes to watch Godzilla movies or do jigsaw puzzles or play with my action figures in my room.

The baby self also has a central role in adult love relationships. In adult life, we can be ourselves in relationships only where we feel that we can get nurtured. It is the difficult paradox of such relationships. We want to be on our best behavior in order to treat our loved ones well. But for the relationship to be nurturing for us, we also need to feel that we do not have to "put on" any behavior, that within the relationship we can act as we feel, not just as we think we should. It is the main challenge for people in long-term relationships—to act considerately while at the same time providing adequate room for the baby self. For without our baby self in a love relationship, we simply cannot get nurtured.

In children, the baby self is especially important and necessary for healthy emotional development. Perhaps the most striking example of this can be seen in a well-known phenomenon with foster children. Many of these children join a new family and are quite well-behaved for a couple of months. But when that "honeymoon period" ends, they start acting badly. The true test of the foster placement follows. Will the foster parents hang in there with the child who is going to give them trouble, or, as often happens, will the agency be called and the child moved on?

But why couldn't these children simply continue being good if their placement was working so well? Certainly they were getting lots of positive feedback and lots of nurturing as a result of their good behavior. Would that not make them want to continue the good behavior? The answer is that they may have been good, they may have been getting lots of positive response, but they were starving. Being on their good behavior meant operating most of the time in the independent mature mode, which is fine, even necessary for most life situations, but not adequate at all for the receiving of primary nurturing. Without primary nurturing to go back to, a child's interest and tolerance for independent activity, a child's capacity and willingness to go out and deal with the world, cannot be sustained.

The baby self, as piggy as it is, is not bad. Only it can get the primary nurturing so necessary for overall well-being. Its presence at home with us, with all of its accompanying unattractive behaviors, does not mean that our child is a monster. In fact, if we are doing a good job as parents, we can know that our child is maturing just fine. We want the baby self to have a time and place and to know that that time and place is with us. We want to give our kids a childhood. They need it. But letting the baby self have its time and place with us also means that parents are stuck with a child who can, will, and must regularly revert to being the craving mindless blob that is the baby self in order to get the special necessary feeding it must have to grow and mature.

The Problem and What to Do about It

There is, of course, a problem. The problem is that the baby self when not getting its way can be a very tough adversary.

For in order to foster growth—mature-self development—parents must set limits and make demands, which the baby self absolutely hates. And against which it will fight tooth and nail. And this is where the tricky part comes in. For if the baby self cannot win, it is just as happy to feed and further provoke as much parent response as it can. Which leaves parents with only one option: *When setting limits and making demands, don't feed the baby self.* Otherwise they risk getting more fussing, bickering, and horrible scenes. These scenes give the baby self the food it craves, but this food does not nourish. This food leads children to hold on and not move forward, it motivates them to repeat the unwanted behaviors in order to get more of the forbidden but terribly tasty food.

A key to effective child raising is to truly believe that it is *not* a problem for our children to misbehave—sometimes—with us and at home. The point of child raising is *not* to stamp out all bad behavior at home, *not* to perfectly shape our children's behavior when they are with us. The point is to make sure that we are putting in all the proper ingredients. Good parenting is treating children well and setting limits and making demands, and then standing back and letting the good processes that we have thereby lodged inside of them grow. If we give them love, don't abuse them, set appropriate limits and make appropriate demands on them, we truly have done what is necessary.

Though we may respond to their baby-self behavior in ways that our children may not like, we are two-faced. On the surface, we react, do what we feel is necessary, but all the while we understand that this behavior is not a big deal. We understand that baby-self behavior does not deserve any *serious* response. If we truly believe that, it frees us to act, and then to swiftly step back, to not get caught up in endless but destructive battles with the baby self. And from this both we and our children reap great benefits. They get their childhood and we get children who behave—most of the time, but not always—and who grow up to be happy and productive adults.

The Wonderful Deal

Letting them have their childhood is part of the wonderful deal. The wonderful deal is that no matter what my children may do, they get everything that I have to give simply because they are my children.

"No matter what I do, I lose nothing just because I was bad? I still get all the good stuff that I would have gotten anyway, no matter what I did? I'm entitled to it? Just because I am me, your darling darlingest? I still get everything, even if Jennifer is better behaved than I am?"

That's the deal. But then Jeremy's sister pipes in.

"You mean even if I'm much better behaved than Jeremy? I don't get any more than him?"

"That's right."

"Then what's the point of my being good?"

"It's your choice."

"Then I'll be bad."

"If you want."

"No matter what I do, good or bad, I get the same as I would anyway?"

"That's the deal. You get the full amount of what we have to give."

"I just get it. Period?"

"That's right."

"So what do I get for being good?"

"We're not mad at you as often as we are at Jeremy. You have more freedom because we can trust you. For example, we can trust you to have paints in your room which we can't do with Jeremy. But that's probably it."

"That's it? That's all I get for being good?"

"That's it. Of course, you get all the good stuff you're entitled to for being our daughter. You automatically get that."

"I can be good or bad and it doesn't make any difference?"

"Yup."

"It's a weird deal."

"Yup."

The whole point is that children like this deal. They love it. They come to feel, at the deepest level of their being, that the deal is a good one. *People, at least Mommy and Daddy, can give just to give. It's not tied into anything that I'm sup-posed to do. They just do it because they want to and they love me.* Having been a recipient of the wonderful deal, having been given to unconditionally, they do not grow into people who seek always to get all they can from everybody but grow into people who can be generous. Having been given to with-out strings, they do not worry about being taken advantage of, and they can trust.

2

Questionable Controls

So if we are not supposed to feed the baby self when we are setting limits and making demands, what does that mean? It means that many normal, healthy, sensible, and—most important—even absolutely good parenting practices are perhaps *not* such good practices. In fact, they often start working against us, producing exactly the opposite of what we are trying to accomplish. Instead of producing positive results, they are greedily devoured by the baby self who then clamors for more.

Being Reasonable and Listening

Most parents today subscribe to the belief that if children are treated well they will thrive—which is absolutely true. Along with this philosophy goes an unspoken assumption that when parents must go against the wants of their children, these same children—because they have been treated kindly, reasonably, with understanding, and are listened to—will respond in a reasonable manner.

"No, Rochelle, you cannot have another lollipop."
"But Mom, I'm really hungry. I really am."
"No, I'm sorry. It's too near dinner. You know how it can spoil your appetite for supper."
"Yeah, I can see your point. I better not have another lollipop."

No way. Not with human children. With human children it sounds a little different.

"No, Rochelle, you cannot have another lollipop."
"But Mom, I'm really hungry. I really am."
"No, I'm sorry, it's too near dinner. You know how it can spoil your appetite for supper."
"But Mom, it's not. It is still over an hour before supper."
"I'm sorry, you'll just have to wait."
"But I can't. My stomach is gurgling. It's true, Mom, my stomach is gurgling. You can hear the gurgling. Put your ear next to it if you don't believe me."
"Rochelle, I am not going to bend down and listen to your stomach."
"See, that's what you always do. You never believe anything I say."
"This is ridiculous, Rochelle."
"No, it's not. Yesterday I told you about Jenny's finger and you didn't believe me, but it was true."
"What has this got to do with Jenny's finger?"
"See, you're not even listening now. I'm talking about how you never listen to me."

We want to be reasonable and we want to listen to them and have them feel "listened to." But reasonableness and listening have their time and place, and that time and place is never when the baby self is in charge and wants to be fed. If we choose to listen under these circumstances, the baby self will very happily give us something to listen to forever.

Yet at times listening is appropriate because children's arguments are not always pure baby-self nonsense. Sometimes they can make sense.

"Jackie, come in the house now."

"Please, Dad. It has been raining the last three days and I'm having such a good time. Please, twenty minutes more. It's not dark yet. Please."

"Okay. Twenty minutes. But no more."

A good rule is to listen to what they have to say one time and, at that point, you can change your mind if you want. Past the first argument, further listening only invites trouble. The fact is, whether we like it or not, extended reasoning and listening do not especially produce children who are reasonable or who feel listened to. Mainly it produces children who are skilled at arguing.

"All the other kids at school will have watched the program, and they'll think I am a jerk because I didn't see it. You always talk about wanting me to have friends from school."

It can be very frustrating. Our excellent arguments, rather than being listened to and thought about, are instead used only as a jumping-off point for their own arguments. Reasoning with children when they are not getting their way may produce solutions, but far more often it just produces more reasons that are, usually, progressively less reasonable but more impassioned.

"Rochelle, do you remember last week? We had chicken fingers which you usually like, and you hardly ate anything. And

it turned out that when you were over at Eva's, you had a big bowl of ice cream."

"But ice cream isn't lollipops. Lollipops are different."

Rochelle's mother will never be able to convince her of the reasonableness in denying her the popsicle.

Another problem with trying to reason with one's children is that these efforts frequently end up such total flops that one cannot help but get angry, frustrated, and disgusted with one's own children. It might happen to Rochelle's mother, in which case she will either give in or more typically get mad at Rochelle.

"I am sick of this, Rochelle. Why can't you just accept what I say. I really get fed up with you sometimes."

Trying to Be Fair

Since the baby self is a very clever self—it employs exactly the same brain as its more mature counterpart—it invariably zeroes in on one particular weak spot of all parents who want to do well by their children.

"Joseph, I want all of those toys picked up now."

"But they're not all mine. Some of them are Richard's."

"I don't care whose they are, I want them all picked up."

"Richard will be home in an hour, why can't he pick up his toys then?"

"I want all of the toys picked up now, and I want you to pick them up."

"Richard never has to pick up any of my stuff."

"Joseph, pick up the toys now!"

"BUT IT'S NOT FAIR."

Fairness is one of the great paradoxes of child raising. It is a very basic and very important principle in dealing with other people, which we truly want our children to understand. Yet it is also the number-one club that children hit their parents over the head with at times of limit setting.

We do want to treat our children fairly, and we do want them to be fair. But in any specific instance where fairness seems to be an issue, parents do not want to worry too much about being fair. Parents do better asking themselves: Am I fair overall? Do I try to be fair? If the answer is yes, then parents should be free not to worry about being totally fair in every instance, because it can't be done and it isn't always important.

Is it fair that Joseph has to pick up his brother's toys? The most appropriate issue here for Joseph's mother is not necessarily fairness at all. Joseph's mother wants all the toys picked up now. She does not want to have to wait until Richard gets home and then, all over again, have to go through the task of getting a child to pick up. It is more convenient and more efficient for her to have Joseph pick up all the toys now. And it is not asking so much from Joseph. Sometimes parents are allowed to give precedence to efficiency over fairness.

Above all, parents do not want to get caught up in fairness arguments. In those arguments, even if fairness were the initial true concern, it gets lost in the "lawyering," and parents find themselves mired in never-ending debates.

"But you let Regina use the spray gun yesterday."
"I know, but it just got too messy."
"But that's not fair. She got to use it."
"I just don't want any mess, Justin. It was a mistake letting Regina use it."
"But how do you know I'll be messy? I deserve a chance."
"I just don't want either of you to use the spray gun."
"But it's not fair. Just because Regina made a big mess that's not my fault."

"You're right, Justin. You didn't get a turn, but I just don't want to take the chance of another mess."
"But then I get cheated."

They could go on forever unless Justin's mother ends it. "I'm sorry. I know it's not fair. But that's the way it's going to be."

"No! It *has* to be fair!" shrieks a disbelieving and outraged Justin, truly ready to take his case to the Supreme Court where he genuinely believes he will win.

"They have to be fair. It's the law, right?"

If fairness as an argument becomes too effective a tool for the baby self, it can get transmuted into something that misses its own point. Fairness can become one of those baby-self principles that become so important in their own right that they must be sought after forever and at all costs, losing their connection to what matters, which in this case is people getting along and finding solutions.

We always want to be fair, but if it is too cumbersome or at times just not possible, one need not worry. After all, in the big, real world, things are not always fair and we want our children to be able to deal with that, too.

Power Struggles—The Battle of Wills

At some point, most toddlers try the following experiment. Their parent says "Come here" (or some similar command) and they say "No." They then watch to see whose orders their bodies will obey, and they discover that their bodies obey them, not their parents. Usually, children find this discovery quite exciting, and they will repeat this—to them—delightful game. Their parents may find it somewhat less delightful.

"Raphael, come here."

"No." Raphael runs off in the other direction squealing with delight.

But prior to the experiment, Raphael really didn't know what would happen or whose will would win. Children are very pleased to see that it is they alone who rule their bodies. Parents can move them around from the outside, but only they can cause their bodies to act. It is the difference between putting Raphael into a car against his will and using threats to make him get into the car by himself. It is orders from the outside versus orders from the inside. With the first, he never did agree to get in the car; with the second, his will loses out and Raphael submits control of his body to his parents' will.

This matter of will, who is in charge of whom, is terribly important to us. By nature, we care intensely that we are the ultimate bosses of our bodies and of what they do. "I am the ultimate boss of me" becomes a very important issue for young children. Most of the time, children feel confident that they are indeed the bosses of their own bodies. Sometimes they just feel the need to reaffirm it.

"Raphael, would you please pick up those crayons?"
"No."
"Raphael!"
"I won't."

Even though Raphael usually is good about heeding requests, on this particular occasion, and for no discernible reason, he absolutely will not pick them up, no matter what.

"I won't."

Raphael stands there and looks straight into his mother's eyes. It is, of course, his re-declaration of independence. *"Just in case you forgot, I am the boss of me."* We want to respect this. The bottom line is that if our children, for no particular reason, absolutely refuse to do something that we want them to do, we do not want to pull out our big guns to bring them into line. We can let them know that we still want them to do it, that we expect them to do it, that we are displeased that they are not doing it, and that there may even be consequences for not doing it. But we do not use our big weapons—big punishments like getting *very* angry or *staying* very angry over a long period of time—to force them to obey.

"Raphael, if you do not pick up those crayons you are going to be in big trouble."

No. Not big trouble. We want to say that if you absolutely refuse, you take your chances about unpleasant consequences, but nothing terrible will happen.

Problems arise only when parents cannot accept that their children might occasionally absolutely defy them. If parents do not truly respect their children's absolute right to be the boss of themselves, then it will become an ongoing issue between them, because children will never let it pass.

"Okay, Raphael, you're in your room and you are not coming out until you pick up the crayons. And I mean it."

The danger is that since Raphael's right as the undisputed ruler of his own body is now seriously challenged, every request can set up a new need for another declaration of independence. Or the field of battle may shift elsewhere—for example, to bowel movements or to eating, where children do have the last word. Or, worst of all, the battle may go underground and breed a deep pool of anger and resentment to be expressed later, elsewhere, and in nasty ways. But normally, children are comfortable that their parents do respect their autonomy.

What we would not want would be the all-too-typical example below.

Cecily, playing with the saltshaker, inadvertently spilled salt on the table. Her mother intervened.

"Cecily, stop playing with the saltshaker. You're spilling salt all over the place. Put it down."

"I'm not hurting anyone."

"You heard me, Cecily. Put down the saltshaker."

"But I don't want to."

"Cecily, put it down."

"No. I won't." Cecily's face assumes a look of determination.

"Put . . . it . . . down!"

"I won't."

"You're asking for it, Cecily."

Her mother's face is now reddening, and her words are coming out through clenched teeth.

Cecily, still just as determined, but tears starting in her eyes, glares at her mother.

"No."

"That's it, Cecily, forget about a treat after supper."

Cecily, herself now bright red, tears coming out, but still glaring, looking right at her mother, throws the plastic salt-shaker across the floor.

"You're really asking for it."

"You're asking for it," glowers Cecily, now having totally abandoned herself to the battle.

At first in a battle of wills, the issue is who gets to rule my body. But once the battle really begins, children cannot help but notice that their saying "no" is important not just to them but to their parent, too. Their parent also cares a lot and wants to win. Children see their defiance as a fight for independence but also something that touches deep inside their parent.

Battles of will, these battles for power, become a rich source of food for the baby self. The baby self feels great power, not because these battles bring parents down to its level, but because the battles elevate the child to the level of the parents. Battles of will also teach that there are two separate wills that cannot exist together. One must triumph. Which is a bad lesson.

In the end, the difference for parents is between being the boss, which is essential, and being bossy, which is not. The difference is control where I have to control everything and control where I am still in charge but can allow for the child's autonomy and separate will. Children who are certain that their parents respect their wills do not have to test that fact constantly. They are thus free to be cooperative—most of the time. Although it's important for children to know that their parents are in charge of their lives, it's equally important for them to know that they are in charge of directing their bodies.

The Baby Self Inside Parents

Just as with children, the baby self in adults does not always willingly stay in its place. A key to effective parenting is to be able to act quickly and then let go. But as you know by now, the baby self never wants to let go, even within adults. More than anything else, this never-wanting-to-let-go characteristic of the baby self wreaks havoc in our adult lives and in the lives of others.

The baby self within us cannot simply put an end to something, cannot drop matters and move on, because doing so makes it feel unsatisfied and incomplete. These are very bad feelings for the baby self, and the baby self can never just accept bad feelings and walk away from them. To get rid of them, it *must* do something. It always wants more, always thinks that there is something more that needs to be gotten, taken care of, finished, resolved, worked through, or better understood. It will not let go.

Picture having just lost money to a vending machine with

nobody there to refund it. The baby self would never leave. It would just keep banging on the vending machine, kicking it, jiggling the coin return. It would wait and wait for that something that would never come.

"*I want you to tell me you're sorry.*"
"*But I don't think I did anything wrong.*"
"*I want you to tell me you're sorry.*"
"*But I can't. I don't feel I did anything wrong.*"
"*You have to.*"

In adults, in parents, the baby self keeps getting hung up on issues that lead nowhere or, worse, to places that are destructive. Yet it feels and genuinely believes that what it is doing is important, that it must be seen through and resolved. But all of these issues are delusions. The only lack of resolution is in one's self, in one's ability to accept what has happened and move on.

The baby self in us cannot accept loss, neither big losses like the death of a family member who is still the center of one's life twenty years later nor little losses like the following.

The restaurant was not his choice. It was not the one he had looked forward to going to. Disappointed that he had not gotten his way, he was unable to forget about it and still enjoy the evening out. Instead, he sulked, ordering unenthusiastically and talking little during the meal.

The baby self in us cannot walk away from arguments. It always wants a resolution that will allow it to avoid any bad feelings.

"But you have to see my side of it. You have to understand how I feel."

Or—

"You have to see that I am right. I have to make you see that I am right."

In parenting, the presence of the baby self can spell disaster.

It can keep parents going when what they should do is stop. Its voice inside the heads of parents often sounds like:

"I just can't let her get away with it. I have to show who is in charge."

"I have to do something about his . . ."

"I need to teach her or else how is she ever going to learn that . . ."

At the behest of the baby self, we cannot merely intervene and then back off, we must also teach them, have them learn, make them understand, make sure that they . . . We feel that we have to change them.

"How many times do I have to tell you. Five o'clock means five o'clock. What is going on in your head that you do not understand that I want you back in the house by then? What is the problem, Kevin? When are you going to learn? Answer me, Kevin!"

When parents go on and on like this, they truly believe that they are acting in the best interests of their child. They believe that there are certain important principles at stake, that certain things must be resolved. But such principles are no more than snares and delusions, traps set by the mindless urgings of the baby self within them. Parents must learn to end things. If they don't, they only give in to the insatiable cravings of the baby self. We need to let go. If we don't, all we do is call out the baby self within our children, who will definitely not let go—a double disaster.

Anna Marie, frustrated by a puzzle she was working on, went over to her mother, who was busy paying bills. Anna Marie demanded that her mother help her with the puzzle.

"I'll help you in a little while, Anna Marie. I'm busy right now."

Anna Marie did not want to wait, and she continued pestering her mother. Her mother finally got quite irritated and ended up putting a tantruming Anna Marie in her room, but not before Anna Marie had gotten pretty nasty.

"You're so mean. You're the meanest mommy. You are. You are."

In her room, Anna Marie sobbed for a while, but then quieted down. Twenty minutes later she was back with her mother.

"Hi," said Anna Marie.

Anna Marie's mother said nothing.

For Anna Marie, it was like a dark cloud coming over the sun. Her mother was still mad at her.

But Anna Marie gave it one more try.

"I made a picture. Do you want to see it?"

This time Anna Marie's mother did respond.

"Anna Marie, you are going to have to learn that every time you want something, you can't just expect people to stop what they're doing and wait on you. You are not the center of the world."

"But you never help me with anything. You never do."

"You know that's not true, Anna Marie."

"It is. You never help me."

"Anna Marie, you'd just better watch it."

The scene deteriorated from there and Anna Marie ended up back in her room. Anna Marie's mother had still been angry at Anna Marie for the nasty things she had said, and for her obnoxious self-centered behavior. She also felt she needed to tell Anna Marie how self-centered she had been. But Anna Marie's mother would have done far better to let matters drop. Having gotten angry at Anna Marie and having sent her to her room, she had already made all the points she needed to make. Parents need to think long and hard before they choose to keep a matter going. Anna Marie's mother accomplished only one thing by continuing. She gave her daughter the message: Things do not go forward, they go back.

Children may misbehave. Parents may have to intervene. Children may respond with tantrums and other horrible behavior. Parents may have to react to that behavior. But then it must end completely and forever. Not to end is a major mistake in child raising, and one for which parents and children will pay heavily. If there were one parenting rule to be etched in stone it would be this: *Things must end.*

The Perils of Teaching

Once upon a time there lived a king and queen who were not happy because, try as they might, they could not have a child. But then one day the queen announced to her husband, the king, "I am going to have a child."

And lo, the proper number of months later the queen gave birth to a beautiful baby girl whom they named Princess Lillyflavor. All were overjoyed and there was much celebrating in the kingdom.

As was the custom with such royal births, on the fifth day after Princess Lillyflavor's birth, all the important people in the kingdom came from near and far to bestow their gifts upon the baby princess, including the most important person of all, the Fairy Dolcemina. Everyone knew her gifts were more precious than diamonds and gold, so when the time came for the Fairy Dolcemina to announce her gifts, the crowd became hushed.

"And to Princess Lillyflavor I give great beauty. And the keenest intelligence. And true kindness."

Unfortunately, just as the Fairy Dolcemina came to the last

gift, the queen had a brief coughing attack and she failed to hear that her daughter had been given kindness as well as beauty and brains.

As the years went by the Princess Lillyflavor grew just as the Fairy had said. She was beautiful and smart. But there was a problem with kindness.

The queen, not having heard the part about kindness, and being the good and concerned mother she was, felt the need to *make sure* that her smart and beautiful daughter would also grow up to be kind. At every possible opportunity she *taught* her daughter about being kind.

"Now don't pet the kitty too hard, dear. You wouldn't want to hurt it."

"Now don't clank your fork too hard when you put it down on the table. You don't want to disturb people with too loud a noise."

"Oh no, dear, pour the juice first for your little friend, Lugwella. She is just as thirsty as you are."

So much did the queen want her daughter to grow up to be kind that in that pursuit—wonderful mother that she was, trying *so* hard—she got to be a bit much. More than a bit much. Princess Lillyflavor had little chance to be kind or anything else because her mother corrected her so swiftly and so often.

"Now Lillyflavor dear, try not to shuffle your feet when you walk. It doesn't offend me but it might offend someone else."

And, as a result of her mother's constant correcting and despite the Fairy Dolcemina's gift of kindness, Princess Lillyflavor grew to hate her mother. She grew to hate her mother so much that, tragically, on the Princess Lillyflavor's twenty-first birthday, she made the following announcement.

"I hate you and I hate Daddy and I hate everybody. I've decided to go off with a group of nasty trolls and ugly witches who roam about the country doing mean things to little children and cute animals. They like me for who I am and they never tell me what to do."

And with that the Princess Lillyflavor left the castle and her parents forever.

And they all lived unhappily ever after.

Moral #1: Don't try too hard or you might lose a battle that you've already won.

Moral #2: Try not to cough when the Fairy Dolcemina grants her gifts.

Parents need to teach their children what is right and what is wrong. Teaching is good. It tells our children what we think and what we believe. It gives them actual verbalized rules to apply to life.

"Reggie, remember to share the cupcakes."

"Candace, it is not good to make fun of other children."

"Now Jordon, remember, it's not good to talk too loudly in restaurants. It will bother people."

These are all good lessons. But if we try too hard, the sum of our behavior becomes the lesson of a parent who controls too much. That's not good and not what we want. We do not have to direct every activity every step of the way.

In our wish to *teach*, we often can also end up in places that we do not want to be. The teacher inside us, though absolutely well-intentioned—*"I have to make them understand"*—goes on and on.

"You're not listening to me, Jacob. Don't give me that look. I'm not getting through to you at all, am I?"

But she is. Jacob has heard his mother. And if his mother has supplied all the other pieces that go into good parenting, Jacob's mature self is listening and is growing just as his mother would want. It is just that his baby self is controlling his current behavior and giving her that "drop dead" look.

Also, sometimes we can miss the point and end up teaching a lesson that we do not want to teach at all, as illustrated in the story of Princess Lillyflavor.

We must never lose sight of this fact: For shaping the character of our children, even more important than what we say to them is how we treat them.

"Candace is our stutter-girl," says her father to his daughter, referring to how sometimes Candace stumbles over her words when trying to get a thought out. Her father means this in good spirit, but Candace is humiliated. She has been told that making fun of others is bad, but that is not what she has learned. Insensitivity begets insensitivity, no matter what we say.

Children take on, as parts of themselves, their parents' values, demands, and restrictions as expressed by the way they are treated. It's a developmental process. This "taking on" will happen *regardless* what parents try to do to make sure that it will happen, *regardless* what they do to make certain that their words and their teachings stick inside their child.

However, though our children take on our values as their own, there is no guarantee that they will keep them. As we mature, our adult self constantly looks at, assesses, reassesses the rules and values we have inherited from our parents. Those rules may be rejected, modified, or reembraced as we come up against them in the context of our own lives.

"My mother always said that being polite to people was very important. But when I was in high school I thought that being polite was being phony. Now I look at it differently and I can see how it is a good way to be."

Teaching is essential. It helps to guide our children. But—especially if we have been good parents—they will also guide themselves.

Rewarding

The use of rewards to produce desired behavior is a time-honored part of child raising.

"Sam, if you eat all your carrots you can have dessert."

"Belinda, if you get all S's or better on your next report card, we will think about getting you the puppy."

"Jacqueline and John-John, if both of you are good the whole time when we are over at Aunt Lenore's, we will go out afterward and get ice cream."

I don't like material rewards as part of child-raising strategy. I think rewards are simply unnecessary. They center child control on getting things. Rewards are the domain of the baby self who seeks only pleasure. The baby self very quickly figures out that if there's no reward, there's no reason to do something. We want to call on the mature self, and the promise of rewards can sabotage its involvement. Material rewards for desired behavior do not produce responsible children. They tend to produce children who want stuff. It's as simple as that.

Harsh Punishment

Harsh punishment—hard slaps across the face, repeated hitting, hitting with belts or with switches, or locking children in a room for extended periods of time, basically doing anything that would cause children to fear their parents—has no place in child raising. And even though today most parents don't use corporal punishment, I'd like to explain why it's so detrimental to children.

One problem with harsh punishment is that the fear instilled in children says to them that there is no excuse for bad behavior. They learn that bad behavior always deserves severe response. There is never any special dispensation or easing of the fullest degree of consequence for being smaller, younger, weaker, more vulnerable, less responsible—in short, *for being a child*. From harsh punishment and its accompanying fear, children learn that there are no excuses for flaws in themselves or in others because they are only *human*.

So much behavior of the baby self fits into a category that would bring harsh punishment into play that harsh punishment also inevitably says to the baby self that it is bad. Many people who have come through harsh childhoods feel that the totally normal healthy baby self inside them is bad. Much that is good inside them and necessary for emotional health comes to be viewed as evil. They see the childish parts of themselves, the fun-loving, impulsive, certainly silly, and naughty parts as bad. Seeing so much inside of them that is forbidden, they can become alienated from themselves. They think they are bad when all they are is normal.

And so they may totally shut themselves down and, like the well-behaved foster children, starve. Unhappy as children, depressed as adults. Or worse, the harshness itself may break out—to be inflicted upon others. The pain that they felt they now deal out upon the world.

Finally, when people come into adult life with the heritage of their own harsh childhoods, they have no sense of where childishness might be okay either within themselves or within others—including their own children. Having never been allowed a childhood, they have no intuitive sense of what it actually is to be a child.

Lesser Punishment

Jeanine's father had bought muffins for a meeting later that day. He put them on the kitchen counter and specifically instructed Jeanine not to eat any of the muffins because he needed them for his meeting. An hour later, Jeanine's father happened to look into the kitchen and saw Jeanine finishing off what turned out to be her second muffin. Her father had told her not to eat the muffins. Now her fate was in her father's hands.

The most obvious response to a crime already committed is normal everyday punishment. A favorite toy is taken away for an afternoon because of constantly hitting one's sister; watching TV is not allowed because of awful behavior at the mall; dessert is missed because of acting up during dinner.

Such punishments are not overly harsh, and sometimes they work, but never perfectly. Under the threat of such unpleasant-but-tolerable punishments, children will behave some of the time and some of the time they will not.

"I warned you that you would lose TV. Now that's it."
"I don't care."

Which of course she does, but the threat is not enough to prevent her from continuing the teasing of her brother during the car ride.

"I told both of you that you would have to behave or else we would not go out to McDonald's. Well, you just lost that."

But even though they did want to go to McDonald's, and they did believe the threat, they just couldn't stop themselves from misbehaving.

Child raising by good and caring parents who use nonharsh punishments produces fairly well-behaved children who then become well-behaved adults. However, this book presents a method of child raising that makes no use of punishment at all, and it also produces fairly well-behaved children who then become well-behaved adults. More or less equally effective systems of child control. Clearly, many wonderful parents using not-overly-harsh punishments have raised many wonderful children. Yet I am not a big fan of punishment.

Punishment is intentionally causing suffering in order to produce child control. That's what punishment is. I think you can raise kids without it.

Is it true that punishment is not needed in raising children, that it is possible to produce the same child-control results without using punishment? Ultimately, the proof is in the pudding. It is how I was raised. It is how my children were raised. Is it possible? Is it better? I can only say that if my readers wish to try it, I think they will be pleasantly surprised.

3

What You Can Do

A Different Kind of Tough

I don't know, this whole deal doesn't sound very tough. I don't want my children walking all over me.

But there is another version of tough, one that very definitely plays tough to both parent and child, one that will keep them from "walking all over me," yet one that has nothing to do with the certain threat of unpleasant consequences. This different kind of tough is the backbone of the system of child control I advocate in this book.

Little Jimmy Barker kept whittling his crayons down to nothing in his crayon sharpener.

"No. You can't do that anymore. That's a waste," said Tex, his father.

But little Jimmy was having a good time sharpening his crayons. And he ignored his father.

Immediately Tex got up, strode over, and took the sharpener away from his son.

"No more sharpening today," said Tex. And Tex put the sharpener high on a shelf that Jimmy could not reach.

"No. I promise. Please. I won't waste, I promise. Please. Give it back."

But Tex said nothing, returning to his work at the big table where he was oiling his guns.

"It's not fair. You're never fair. You're a jerk," sobbed and screamed his infuriated son.

But Tex just gave his quiet smile and continued with his work, briefly stopping to stare out the front window, looking across the vast prairie.

Another story:

One day Tex and little Jimmy rode into town. As a special treat, they stopped in at Ol' Pete's General Store, where Tex bought Jimmy four wooden soldiers. But when they got home Jimmy realized that he had left one of his soldiers' little wooden guns back at the store. He had a fit.

"We have to go back to the store. We have to go back to the store. I need my other wooden gun," sobbed Jimmy.

The town was a forty-minute horse ride away, and Tex was going back the next day anyway. Also, Tex had a lot more guns to oil.

"No. Sorry, little fella. I ain't going back today. I'll get it tomorrow."

"But you have to," screamed little Jimmy. "You have to."

But Tex just sadly shook his head.

"Sorry, little fella."

"No! You have to! You have to!"

And Jimmy started shrieking at the top of his lungs and kicking everything in sight. But Tex only kept on oiling his guns and staring out across the vast prairie.

It is a tough parent who can say, "I am the boss, the one who is in charge. I decide what happens and there is *nothing* you can do to change that. I love you, but your power is limited. I am the parent and you are the child."

I think many parents are uncomfortable presenting the idea that the ultimate basis of their authority with their children is that *they*, the parents, are the boss. But here they make a mistake. Parents are in charge not because they are wiser, not because all their decisions are right, but because they are the parents. I can let my children make decisions—for example, "Tonight you get to decide when you go to bed." But it is I who let them make that decision. I am the captain of this ship. Sometimes an easy captain. Sometimes a strict one. But I remain in charge.

There is no reason to obscure the fact that I am the parent, and until you are an adult, you are stuck with me in charge. That is exactly what children want and absolutely need to hear. Children ultimately do accept our right to boss them around, not because they are so convinced that we know so much more than they, but because they love us—even though they don't always agree with us—and because they find considerable security in the fact that there is a bigger, stronger person in their lives. Children need to feel that their parents, not they, are the boss. Parents need to feel it too.

How It's Done

Okay, I am the boss and I make the decisions. But how do I do it?

There are two basic rules.

First, if you are going to take any parental action or make

any decision that may conflict with the wants of your child, do it *fast*. Say "Yes" or say "No," but don't drag it out. If you allow the process to drag on, the baby self will move in. Problems arise when the baby self manages significantly to draw out the process in some way—through temper tantrums, repeated begging, abject pathos, or endless arguing—and this sustained onslaught has some effect. *That* is a disaster.

> "Can I stay up late tonight and watch another program?"
> "No, I don't think so, James. Not tonight."
> "But please. Just this time. It's really a good program."
> "No, I am sorry, James."
> "I promise I won't ask again for a long time."
> "No, I am sorry, James. You need the sleep."
> "No, I don't. I won't get tired."
> "You've said that before, but I know how tired you can get."
> "But I won't this time. And it's a really special program. You never let me do anything special."
> "That's not true, James."
> "Yes it is. When was the last time I got to do anything special?"
> "I don't know, James. But we do let you have special things sometimes."
> "Name one."
> "Oh, for goodness sakes, James. Don't you ever give up? Go ahead. Watch the program. Be tired in the morning."

No. Far too long. Much better would have been:

> "Can I stay up tonight and watch another program?"
> "No, I don't think so, James. Not tonight."
> "But please. Just this time. It's a really good program."
> "No, James. Not tonight."
> "But please. It's really special. It is. You never let me do anything special."

But by that point James's father should have permanently exited from the discussion.

Or let him stay up.

"Can I stay up special tonight and watch another program?"
"Oh, I guess so. Okay."

Let him stay up. Don't let him stay up. It doesn't matter. What does matter is that whatever you decide, whatever you do, do it fast.

But what if a parent cannot decide quickly?

Then decide quickly to postpone the decision.

"Mom, can I have a hamster?"
"I don't know, dear. I'll have to think about it."
"Please can I have one. I'll take good care of it. I promise I won't let it die like the last one. Please."
"Ivan, I said I would think about it."
"Please, Mom, please. Can I? Can I?"
"I said I would think about it."

Which is a good answer. It is firm. It is making a decision—that I will not decide now. You are not letting them pester you into a decision that you are not ready to make and it accomplishes what you want in bringing a swift end to the decision-making process.

At a time of your choosing you can return to the question. But for the time being, the matter has been closed quickly.

Whatever you do, do it fast.

The second rule, and perhaps the harder of the two, is that once you have made your decision, you must stay with that decision for the duration.

In the convenience store Justin wanted some bubble gum.

"No, Justin, no gum."

"Please, please. Just once."

"No, I am sorry, Justin."

"Please, please. Just one time. Please, please."

And Justin, overly tired and probably needing a nap, not bubble gum, then really started fussing and whining, eventually working himself into a full-fledged tantrum which his mother knew could go on for a long time.

"I want gum. I want gum," sobbed Justin, now literally rolling on the floor in despaired outrage.

Having taken a firm stand, Justin's mother has to stay with her decision. These are the battles that count and parents need to win. They do win them if they stay with their decision. Justin's mother's ability to endure the tantruming—no matter how far Justin takes it—says to Justin, "You can misbehave, but your behavior will get you nowhere. That is the key point: Their behavior cannot change a decision.

If You Are Not Up for a Battle

Where you truly make a stand, the baby self must never win or ever wear you down. Full-scale battles with baby selves can be very wearing, so if you're not up for it, don't battle.

Four-year-old Arnold's mother was tired and had no energy to battle her son. She had had an unusually long, hard day. Just before dinner Arnold came up to his mother.

"I want a cookie."

Normally Arnold's mother would have said "No." Snacks before supper interfered with his eating. But Arnold's mother sighed deeply. She knew Arnold, and she knew, especially by his tone of voice, that if she said no she was in for a prolonged tantrum. Arnold's mother did not feel like having to go through one of these. She just didn't have the patience or energy for it.

"Sure, Arnold," said his mother with feigned perkiness as she gave him his cookie.

But didn't Arnold's mother make a mistake? Wasn't she allowing herself to be bullied by the potential threat of a tantrum? Wasn't she thereby playing directly into the hands of Arnold's baby self? Wasn't she also going against one of her standing rules?

Had Arnold's mother taken a stand against the cookie, she might not have had the patience to withstand one of his huge screaming temper tantrums and might have given him the cookie midtantrum. The tantrum would have worked.

Or, worse, Arnold's mother might have blown up at him.

"I've had it with your tantrums. When are you going to learn to accept 'No' as an answer. I have had it with you, Arnold."

The baby self licks its lips and will most assuredly come back another day for more. It has won big time and gotten the special passionate feeding that it so adores.

Save your firm stands for when you are up to it. Firm stands must sometimes be taken. But pick the times when you are ready and able to see a battle to its end. And the times when the setting is right. At the home of an elderly aunt where Arnold's mother *really* did not want to have him throw a tantrum, she let him have the cookie.

Or in the car at the start of a dreaded three-hour car ride, where there is no way of getting distance between oneself and the tantrum thrower. We cannot say:

"That's it, Arnold, get out of the car."

"You're going to leave me here on the Interstate?"

Let him have the cookie.

Or if Arnold's mother was in a big hurry to get somewhere and a tantrum was the last thing she needed. There the time constraint gives Arnold too much power. Give him the cookie.

And not just the time and the setting.

Sometimes we simply don't care enough about their behavior to take a firm stand.

"Elena, do not touch the curtains!"

Elena, acting as though she had not heard, kept tugging at the curtain anyway.

And Elena's mother just continued reading her book without another word to her daughter.

We may not always feel like getting up and going over and stopping Elena from pulling at the curtain. We may not think it is worth the effort. *She can't pull it down. She can't get hurt. And I really don't feel like getting up.* Sometimes we just are not going to follow up on what we say. And this is fine provided we really don't care whether Elena pulls at the curtain or not. Sometimes we may care but not enough, and so we choose not to take a firm stand because there are other things about which we care more—for example, were Elena to start pulling at an electric cord.

All of which means that parents must pick and choose which decisions to be steadfast about, when they have the patience, the energy, when the circumstances permit it, or when they truly care.

You Can Change Your Mind

Parents want to make a decision and not back down, but these rules are more flexible than you might at first think. For example, you *can* change your mind. However, any change must happen early on in the decision-making process, and it has to happen swiftly. Then, the decision *must* be final. Here are a few examples:

Parents are allowed to change their minds on a whim.

"Can I have another cookie?"
"No, Helena, two is enough."

"Please!"

"You know, I am in such a good mood today, I don't think I am going to say no to anything. Sure. Have another cookie."

"You're not going to say no to anything?"

"Nope."

"Can I get a pony?"

I reiterate what I said earlier about listening. Parents may change their minds because their child's initial counterargument does make sense.

"Can I have another cookie?"

"No, Helena, two is enough."

"But you said supper was going to be a lot later tonight. And I'm going to get real hungry."

"Oh, okay, Helena. You can take another."

But I also remind you that parents proceed at their own peril if they listen past the first argument.

Parents may change their minds if they perceive that it is something special for their child. They can make an exception because it is something that their child wants very much.

"Okay, you can stay up the extra half hour. I know the 'Dynamo Worm Full Hour Special' means a lot to you."

Exceptions like this are in fact particularly good because they give a nice message: "I know and care about what is special to you, and what makes you happy is such a high priority with me that I can sometimes make exceptions to the rules." Your willingness to change your mind says you care about how your child feels and what he says can have an effect. But only up to a point. Once the final decision is made, a parent absolutely, totally, without questions, wants to convey that, past that decision, *nothing* that their children do or say will have an effect.

Consistency

What? How can you ever be consistent if you pick and choose and if you change your mind? Aren't parents supposed to be consistent? Doesn't that contradict all the rules of good parenting?

No. Parents do not have to be consistent, but they must consistently be the decision-makers. They do not have to be consistent either in deciding the same thing time after time or in having rules always the same from place to place and person to person.

Very early, children perceive quite accurately that rules with a given parent do differ from situation to situation. And not just rules with one parent. Different rules for each parent, and for other people, and for different places.

"When Mommy is in a good mood I can ask her for stuff. But when she is in a bad mood, forget it."

"Mommy gets mad if I bang the furniture with my drumsticks. Daddy doesn't care at all."

"We get in trouble if we make a lot of noise at Grandma Levin's. But at Nana and Poppop's, we can go wild."

Children are not stupid. We can give them many rules for their behavior, instructions about what behavior is acceptable and what is not. But what they learn are the real rules.

"I do not want you pestering your sister."

But the reality is, "If I pester Tricia, Mommy tells me to stop but doesn't do anything unless me and Tricia start screaming at each other, which is when Mommy gets real mad and actually does something."

Hence the real rule: "You *can* pester Tricia, until it gets out of hand." Which is most parents' rule, and is actually a perfectly good one where siblings are concerned.

Through trial and error, children learn the reality of your rules, the reality of when you will decide to intervene. What makes Daddy mad. What makes Daddy very mad. What would cause Daddy to get up and actually do something rather than just yell. They learn to differentiate. Limits with Mom. Limits with Dad. Limits at home. Limits when we are in a restaurant. Limits at school. Limits with friends. Limits with Caroline, the baby sitter. Different limits with Sherri, the other baby-sitter. Of course, this corresponds to the real world where there *are* different limits, different rules with different people and in different places.

In child raising, what matters is not that the decisions always be consistent but that the decision maker consistently be the parent, not the child.

But What If I'm Wrong?

But if I'm making all these decisions, especially so quickly, what if I'm wrong? I don't want to make decisions that in the end are going to hurt my child.

A major fact in making decisions in day-to-day child raising is that we do not always have to do the right thing. We can make mistakes. The trick is in being comfortable that you are the right person to make the decisions. Which means that sometimes we are allowed to be wrong. The basis of parental control is not in our infallibility but in the fact of our being the parent. What if we had a child who was smarter than we? Should we turn decision making over to him or her?

"But, Dad, an article in last month's New England Journal of Medicine *showed that children who demand large quantities of cookies before supper may be hypoglycemic (too low blood sugar) and need the sugar. How can you know I'm not hypo-glycemic? We certainly can't get me tested between now and supper."*

"Gosh, Marcus, I don't know what to say. Your point is well taken. Here's the bag of cookies."
"Thanks, Dad. You're an excellent father."

As parents, we have the responsibility of making a life for our children, which means making a thousand decisions, day in, day out. It just does not work to have to fully consider everything, to listen to everyone, to expect ourselves to be totally wise and fair and not to make mistakes. It cannot be done.

Our children sink or swim not so much with the wisdom of our decisions—we can only do what we think best—but with our comfort and confidence in our role as their parent and decision maker.

Making Your Decisions Stand

Early Controls

"Jason, get in the car."

Jason laughs and runs in the other direction. If we want Jason in the car, we have to run after him, pick him up, and put him in the car.

In early childhood, if you want it done, you get up, go over, and do it. If you really want something to happen, you must make it happen. If you really want something *not* to happen, you must make sure that it *cannot* happen. You make a decision to act and then act quickly. A baby reaches for a hot stove and her father pulls her hand away; a plastic hammer that is being used to bang a brother is taken away; a child too close to the street is pulled back. Action, not words, is the foundation of early child control. It is the most basic of controls.

Our highest priority is always to prevent anything that might risk serious harm to our children or others. Medicines or breakables are taken out of reach. Young children are not left alone near the street or with their newborn baby sister, whom they love dearly but whom they might nonetheless wish to examine to see how soft the soft spot on her skull really is.

In early childhood, these are the two basic controls: before-the-fact prevention, and actual physical prevention. These are all that a parent needs or can rely on. The number-one mistake of early child raising is when parents too much want their words to control their child. It simply doesn't work. If a parent does not like what is going on, and if the child does not respond *immediately* to words, the parent should—right away—intervene.

The bottom line is that with small children if you want something obeyed, you had better be ready to act. Early and swiftly. And as discussed, if you are not so certain that you care enough to actually get up and do something—"Darryl, stop tickling Daniel"—then you had best be prepared that maybe you will be obeyed but maybe you won't.

But if you care, you must act. Fast. How do you know if you care enough that you should act? If you *start* to get irritated, that's when to act.

A good rule is that if one's child is doing something that one genuinely wants him to stop doing, say it *once*. That's all. And if he does not immediately stop doing whatever he is doing, then go over and stop him. Pull him away from the lamp. Take away the scissors. And do it quickly.

If parents complain, "Why do I have to tell you three or four times before you will listen?" it is they who are at fault. They should have acted after the first time. Or recognized that, if such is the case, they really do not care enough to do anything about it.

The beauty of this strategy, and it is the main trick of

early child raising, is that it saves much parental wear and tear. And it gets results. Children learn "If my mom means it, she acts—fast." And, far more often than not, they do respond.

"Jason, keep out of my desk drawer."
"Okay, okay."

Jason moves away from the desk, seeing his mother poised to get out of her chair and come over and pull him away.

The problem with this strategy is that it does require continuing physical effort. There is no substitute. But if parents learn, where they care, to act—right away—they will be pleased to find that they end up having to act a whole lot less.

But what if they keep doing it, even after I stop them? What if they keep being obnoxious?

The bottom line of physical intervention is separation of parent and child. The removal to elsewhere, often referred to as "time-out." But separation is not a punishment. As soon as children can control themselves, they can come back. They are welcome back, if they can behave.

"Hi. Can I come back?"
"Of course."

If they do not behave, out they go again. But they are still welcome back. Only with repeated reentries with continued fussing—or where it is obvious that they are out of control—need the banishment extend over time.

"No, Matthew. I think you need to stay in your room for a while."
"No! No!"

The hysterical Matthew is again carried to his room. But this time he's there to stay for a while, not as punishment but as a statement of fact: As long as you continue to fuss, it will not be around me. Children learn to understand this difference. They *can* come back if they can control themselves. In fact, when they've learned the difference, they usually will only do battle when they are really out of sorts.

But what if they refuse to separate? What if they keep coming back?

This final leverage—separation—is so much the initial bottom line to effective child control that the answer is that you must stay with it. Even if that becomes a long, wearing process, you have to put in the time and the effort. In the end it is worth it.

One night, when my son Nick was just under two years old, he discovered how to climb out of his crib. He was excited by his discovery, and instead of lying in his crib and going to sleep, which is what he usually did, he kept climbing out of his crib and toddling in to see Mary Alice and me.

"No, Nick, you have to stay in bed." And one or the other of us would pick him up and carry him back to his crib. But he kept climbing out and we kept putting him back.

"No, Nick, bedtime."

At last he gave up. I guess he was either finally bored with his new skill or maybe just tired. But before he quit, he had gotten out of bed fifteen or twenty times. The same thing happened the following night. Perhaps there were not quite so many trips, but still a lot. For about a week, we were stuck with Nick's coming out of his crib and our carrying him back to it. But there was no other choice. A fact of being a parent of a young child is that it requires continuing physical effort, for which there is no substitute.

Yelling, threatening, cajoling, or even sitting with him until he got sleepy would have been a disaster. Those tactics would have taught Nick, "If I get out of bed, I can get more involvement from Mommy and Daddy." Who knows for how many nights, or years, the getting-out-of-bed may have continued.

"I'm thirsty."
"I can't sleep."
"My tooth hurts."

Parents' Wishes—Parents' Displeasure

As children get older, there comes a gradual shift away from physical intervention as the major source of control until ultimately it no longer has any role at all.

"Armando"—who is fifteen years old, six feet one, and 185 pounds—"get in the car," says his mother, who is five feet two and 111 pounds. "No? Then I will just have to put you in."

Not exactly the way it works.

Physical intervention is replaced by a number of other child controls, all of which have one thing in common: The wishes, the approval, and the disapproval of parents are the bases of that control. They aren't always totally reliable, but they are very powerful controls and they are enough.

Three-year-old Luke, intentionally disobeying his mother, splashed water from his bath onto the bathroom floor.

Luke's mother, not amused, spoke to him angrily.

"No, Luke. That's enough. You can splash in the tub, but not on the floor."

Luke did not splash water out of the tub for the rest of his bath, nor did he the next time he took a bath. And at its end, he said to his mother, "See, I didn't splash the floor. Aren't I good?"

Eight-year-old Marcie, sitting on the floor near her father, had been playing with her Toga Blocks. But no longer interested, she went on to do something else.

"Marcie, now that you are finished with your Toga Blocks, why don't you put them away?"

"I'm too tired."

"Marcie, I want you to put away the Toga Blocks."

"I'm too tired."

And Marcie flopped on the floor demonstrating how tired she was.

"Marcie, I want you to put away the Toga Blocks."

"I'm too tired."

This time Marcie spoke in a particularly tired and whiny voice, as she simultaneously collapsed her body even further, so as to even more poignantly plead her case of absolute exhaustion.

Her father said nothing.

"I'm too tired."

"I really *am* tired," said Marcie, this time quite grumpily, as she struggled to her feet dragging herself over to the Toga Blocks, which she then nicely put away.

"Thank you, Marcie," said her father.

Obviously, not all such situations work out as smoothly as these two. Sometimes, they do not work out at all. But the above stories are not sheer fantasy. This is the way that children will react in many situations if a parent were to do no more than what the parents in these stories did.

State a demand, repeat it, and say nothing more.

Let's look at Marcie's example more closely. She did not feel like picking up her blocks, but her father said that he wanted her to. Now she felt pressure from her father to do so even though she still didn't want to. His want, this unpleasant intrusion, sat inside her head, interfering with her pleasant afternoon. She would have been quite content to go off and play with something else, totally ignoring the unpicked-up blocks.

"I'm tired," she had said, grasping at what first came into her mind as a possible means—not that she really expected it to work—of somehow canceling out her father's request.

But it would not go away. Had she been in a particularly stubborn or lazy mood she might have toughed it out, absolutely refusing to pick up the blocks. But on this occasion Marcie capitulated and picked up the blocks. She chose the unpleasant strain (not really all that unpleasant) of actually picking up the blocks over the continuing unpleasantness inside her head of her father's unmet demand.

The result was that her unpleasant feelings were gone immediately and maybe in the bargain she received some approval from her father. An absolute and invariable result of children having made an attachment to a parent is that they care about the parent, and care about how the parent feels toward them. If parents are happy with them, they are happy. If parents are displeased with them, it bothers them, even if they say it doesn't. They do care even though they often say they don't.

"Stephanie, I asked you this one time not to make a mess in the living room, and you did. I am very mad at you."
"I don't care."

But she does care. That is the whole point. She cannot help but care. *They always care.*

Children say, "I don't care," but not because they do not care, but rather in a wishful attempt to exorcise the evil, disapproving presence inside of them, or to get back at their parent, at whom they are now angry for making them feel bad. But only time or parents' saying they are not angry anymore can diffuse the unwanted disapproving presence.

The fact that children do care about what their parents

think—and cannot do otherwise—is the number-one tool that parents have in controlling their children. A primary reason that children behave is that they do not want to risk their parents' displeasure. What many parents do not realize or tend grossly to underestimate is the very real power that their wants have over their children. All too often they never give it a chance. They never get to know that quiet kind of power, to experience it, to understand it as a very real ally in getting their children to do what they want them to do.

Let's say Marcie's father had chosen a different way to try to get Marcie to pick up her blocks.

"Marcie, now that you are finished with the blocks, why don't you put them away?"

"I'm too tired."

"Marcie, I want you to put away the Toga Blocks."

"I'm too tired."

"Marcie, you can put away the Toga Blocks or you can miss TV for the rest of today."

Maybe this would get Marcie to put away the blocks and maybe it would not. But perhaps if Marcie's father had not used the threat and had said nothing more, as in the first example, Marcie would have put away the blocks. In the second example Marcie's father will never get to know if his just making the demand would have had the desired result all on its own.

Very often all most parents have to do once they have stated what they want is nothing. And to sometimes do this, and to see that it—just their wanting their child to behave in a certain way—has a very real power over their child, is a valuable lesson to parents.

Guilt

Ruthy's mother asked her daughter a number of times to pick up her Construct-O-Straws from in front of the television. They were going out and Ruthy's mother wanted it done now. She did not want to wait. So after one last unresponded-to request, she picked up the Construct-O-Straws herself.

Ruthy's mother then turned to her daughter and spoke to her angrily.

"I did not like that. When I ask you to do something, I expect you to do it. I just had to pick up your Construct-O-Straws. It was your job, not mine. And you didn't do it."

And with that, she turned and walked out of the room.

So what? Ruthy got away with not picking up the Construct-O-Straws.

Ruthy did not get away with anything. Her mother's words—because of the inevitable love attachment—made her feel bad. Guilty.

And the proof is that rarely after such a rebuke will the Ruthies of the world remain silent.

"I was going to. You just didn't give me a chance. You never give me a chance."

The words made her feel guilty. And she was left stewing in the guilt. Though probably not for too long. And next time maybe she will pick up the Construct-O-Straws and maybe she will not. But the guilt she might feel if she does not do it will put a real pressure on her to comply.

A system that does not use punishment relies heavily on guilt as a control. Children are made to feel uncomfortable because they did something they were not supposed to do.

But isn't it bad to make them feel guilty all the time? Isn't that the way you make neurotic children?

There are many situations where children *should* feel guilty. Like in the above example. Or if they have done something intentionally or unthinkingly that caused harm or aggravation, and as a result somebody is upset at them, they should feel guilty. It's okay for them to feel guilty if, for example, they kept pestering you when your friend was visiting and you got mad, or if they were asked to help put away the Christmas tree decorations and stubbornly refused, or if they were told not to wrestle on the couch, which they did anyway and bumped the lamp, which fell and broke.

In such situations children *should* feel guilty. If they do, that guilt will influence them in the future not to do it again. If they feel guilty they will have to learn to deal with guilt. After all, it's one of the unpleasant feelings that life gives us that we all have to learn to handle.

However, since they are children, the quantity of guilt that they can handle is limited. Guilt that is too heavy-handed doesn't teach them anything productive because it either gets blocked out altogether or simply overwhelms them.

"Look what you've done. Now your father and I are fighting because of you."

Too terrifying: *"Am I going to cause a divorce?"*

"I told you not to wrestle on the couch and now see what's happened."

But this time it was not a lamp, but his brother Chad's nose which smashed against a table and was broken in a welter of blood.

Again, too terrifying. One wants to soften it some.

"I told you not to wrestle on the couch because this is the kind of thing that can happen. I know that you didn't mean for Chad to break his nose. That was an accident."

This way, some guilt is handed out for the wrestling on the couch, but not for the consequences, since the broken nose was unintentional. The child is not made to feel responsible for the broken nose and all the blood.

"I asked you two to try to play quietly, but you just couldn't. And now I have a headache and I still have to make supper and finish the laundry and straighten up. It's just real hard on me."

No. Not. Again, it is too much. It is too much for children to feel responsible for their parents' welfare. That is their parents' job.

Far better would be:

"I asked you two to play quietly. But you just couldn't. Now I have a headache. Couldn't you just once play together without squabbling?"

They may feel guilty, but the parent in the second version is holding her own. *She* is dealing with her headache while also being angry, but she's not weighing down her children with the full responsibility for her suffering. *That* would be too much guilt.

But guilt used appropriately is a powerful child control. And a very useful one.

Getting Angry

Jessica's mother told her not to go into the flour canister. But when her mother was out of the room Jessica did, and in the process spilled flour all over the counter. When Jessica's mother returned and saw the mess, she immediately started yelling at her daughter.

"Now look at this mess. I told you not to touch the flour. Have you no sense? What is your problem, Jessica? I told you not to touch the flour. Look at this mess. Just look at it."

And Jessica—upset by the angry tirade—started to cry.

Randolph's father was busy working in the kitchen. Randolph, bored and with nothing better to do, kept tugging at his father's pant leg.

"What is it, Randolph?"

Randolph said nothing but continued his tugging. Randolph's father, irritated, grabbed his son a little more roughly than he might have intended and said angrily, *"Randolph, now stop that."*

Randolph began to cry.

Is it all right to get angry at one's children? Can parents' anger damage children? Is it always preferable for parents to use an alternative other than anger? For example, is it always better to say things like:

"Jessica, I told you not to touch the flour canister. Now you did, and there is a big mess that has to be cleaned up."

Or—

"Randolph, I know you are bored. Let's try to think of things you can do."

Anger is a normal and healthy reaction to unpleasant situations. For better or for worse, it is built in as part of the package of being a human. An essential part of mental health is the capacity to feel and express anger where it is appropriate. But also important—in order to be able to deal with the real world successfully—is the ability to handle *other people's* anger.

Does parents' anger damage children? Is parents' anger in some way traumatic for children, causing emotional hurt that will leave a scar? Yes, if the anger is too intense, or too constant. Yes, if the child is too young to be exposed to anger. One does not yell at babies or ever intentionally handle them roughly. And yes, very definitely yes, if anger turns into physical violence. *Then* any anger becomes damaging.

But can children out of babyhood handle the normal—not violent, not excessive—angry parent? Yes. Does that anger damage them? It does not seem to.

Parent Anger and Parent Violence

Valerie, six, was bored and had asked her mother if she would play Go-for-the-Bunny with her. Her mother said no, she was too busy. But Valerie persisted and persisted to the point where her mother got quite aggravated. And still Valerie carried on.

"But why not? Why not?"
"Valerie, I said no, and I mean it."
"But you never do anything for me. You never do. You're a fat jerk."

Valerie's mother exploded, her face turned red and she started screaming at her daughter.

"Valerie, I am sick and tired of your mouth. I am sick of it."

Twice she smacked Valerie hard across the face.
A different version of the story.

"But why not? Why not?"
"Valerie, I said no, and I mean it."
"But you never do anything for me. You never do. You're a fat jerk."

Valerie's mother exploded.

"Valerie, I am sick and tired of your mouth. I am sick of it. You understand? I am sick of it. Sick of it. I've had it with you. I've had it. When are you going to learn to behave? When are you going to learn some respect? I'm sick of this. Sick of it. Just sick of it."

Valerie, under the onslaught, burst into tears and ran from the room.

Versions one and two are parts of two separate worlds. In version two, Valerie's mother, out of control as she was, raving as she did, upsetting to Valerie as it must have been, limited her anger to words. Yes, Valerie's mother should not have gotten as angry as she did. Yes, she should have handled the scene differently by removing Valerie earlier when she started to get angry. But we are not always going to handle situations as we should, especially with in-your-face-type children. Sometimes our patience—through no fault of our children's—may be nonexistent. Yes, it is not ever good to rave at our children. But the big issue, the huge issue, is where we draw the line on our own behavior. In the second version, Valerie's mother, angry as she was, put limits on her anger. Raving, yes, but violent, no. There is a world of difference between yelling and screaming and physical violence. The most important issue is not whether parents show anger, it is whether that anger turns into violence.

As awful as her mother's anger must have been for Valerie, if it went only that far and never further, she knows her mother's limits: *Mad as I get at you, I will not cross over that line. I will not harm you. I will not.* So long as children know that the anger will not lead to violence, so long as they know the anger will not hold over and will not cause any loss of love, so long as the anger is part of the larger context of "my parents do unequivocally love me, they will do all they can to protect me," then parents' anger does not harm children. It upsets them for the moment, but they can get over it without scars.

Perhaps children even learn something important from nonviolent, not-excessively-angry, not-grudge-holding parental anger. They can learn that other people's anger, provided it does not turn into violence, can be something that is simply not that terrible. It makes you feel bad, but the bad feeling goes away in a little while. Over time, children can learn to deal with other people's anger.

Parents often feel that if they have allowed themselves to get angry they have failed. "I know I shouldn't let myself get mad, but sometimes I just can't help it. He can be *so aggravating*." But it's inevitable. Parents do get angry at their children. I am not saying parents *should* get angry at their children. But I am saying that if parents get angry at a child and show it in the normal course of raising a child, it is not a problem. The problem, the very big problem, is where anger turns into violence.

Put-Downs—Name-Calling

"Germaine, you're so stupid. I can't believe you did that."

Nobody—not adults, not kids—ever likes or responds other than badly to any kind of name-calling. Name-calling—where we say something negative about *them* rather than about what they did.

If what he did was stupid, say that *what he did* was stupid. Do not say that *he* is stupid.

"Germaine, I can't believe you left the ice cream out. That was so stupid."

It may seem like a small point, but it is not.

If we call people stupid, what are they supposed to do?

Mom says I'm stupid. What does she want me to do, grow a better brain?

If we say what they *did* was stupid, at least the next time—if they want—they can try to be more thoughtful.

Of course, with normal day-to-day parenting sometimes we will name-call. And if it is not too often, our children can handle it. But it is never good.

Separation

Separation is the bottom line in early child control. If a child continues to act in a manner that we find unacceptable, the child is banished or removed—until he or she can act in a more acceptable manner. But separation is also the bottom line in later child control, and even for conflicts in adult life.

The essence of separation is that the nurturing parent is simply no longer there, no longer available for the baby self to feed on or to make things better. But as children get older there are ways of accomplishing separation other than making *them* go elsewhere, as in early childhood. For example, *you* can be the person to leave.

"No, Yvette, you cannot go out tonight," says Yvette's mother to her fifteen-year-old daughter. "We have been all over this before. It's a school night and you went over to your friend's last night. The answer is 'No.' And I don't want to hear any more about it."

But Yvette wants her mother to hear a lot more about it.

"But I have to. You're being totally unreasonable."

Yvette's mother turns on her heels and walks away, and Yvette follows, not letting up, even when her mother goes into another room, closing and locking the door between them to keep Yvette away. Yvette presses her face to the door.

"You *have* to."

Yvette has not given up, but separation has been established. If Yvette cannot reengage her mother, the separation works.

"You're really being unreasonable," screams Yvette. But now she retreats from her hopelessly nonunderstanding mother to go to her room to call her friend and complain to her. Only when Yvette is separated does she begin to calm down and start to accept the fact that she cannot go out.

Although our main concern in this book is children, let's take a quick look at how crucial separation becomes in arguments between adults. Once an argument has reached a certain emotional level with naked baby selves flailing at each other, each of them wanting a concession or a retraction from the other, separation is the only way to end things. Only when the combatants separate, cool down, and think clearly about the situation will their conflict have a chance at resolution.

"She's right, there's no real reason why I shouldn't help with the dishes. But she still does nag too much."

All too often, if they do not separate, one or the other combatant ends up saying things that they wish they had not—too hurtful—or, worse, the argument ends in violence.

There is one last important form of separation—nonresponse, which is where one does not pick up on any attempts at provocation, where one ignores certain behavior. For parenting especially, nonresponse is such an important tool that it deserves its own separate discussion later in this chapter. But first let me talk about a form of behavior control that certainly looks just the opposite.

Nagging

If you want children to do something that they do not feel like doing, there are many options. But unfortunately there are not many that will work consistently. One may try cute strategies.

"Come on now, let's play a game. Let's see if you can pick up all your toys before I count to seventy-three. I'll bet you can't."

"Hee, hee, hee," squeals little Franz, as he plunges into the task while his father slowly counts, "thirteen . . . fourteen. I don't think you can do it."

"Hee, hee, hee," squeals little Franz as he sees that he will win.

Sometimes, when the task is too big, we may want to participate.

"Erika, I want you to pick up your room."
"I can't."
"Erika, I want you to pick up your room now."
"I can't."

In fact, six-year-old Erika's room was in a state of major mess. Clothes, toys, many tiny things were strewn about, covering the entire floor. It *was* a big task.

"Come on, Erika, I'll help."

Erika's father sat down on the floor and began the process of sorting through the mess, figuring out where the different items could go. Erika joined him and over the next half hour they picked up her room. It was a big job. It may genuinely have been beyond Erika's ability even to know where to start.

Sometimes it is useful to work with children, in effect supporting their effort to do unwanted tasks. But ultimately one is stuck with the harsh reality.

"Come on, Franz, pick up your toys."

Little Franz ignores his father.

"Come on, Franz, it's time to pick up your toys."
"Can't I play just a little more?"

"Franz, I want you to pick up your toys. Now."
"I'm tired. I'm ti-ered."
"Pick up the toys now."
"I can't."
"Franz, pick up your toys."
"Oh, all right."

And little Franz unhappily picks up the toys.

That's called *nagging* and a frequent bottom line with children is that if you do not nag, it will not happen. If you care enough about something, nagging is a good strategy. Sometimes they will absolutely refuse. We'll talk about that shortly. But most of the time they will acquiesce to your wishes. They just do not want to do it and will hold out, not with flat-out refusal but with the 6,001 ploys of the baby self. They desperately hope they can wait out their parents. But if parents hang in there they usually will prevail because, ultimately, most children will do what is asked of them most of the time.

"Melanie, how many times do I have to tell you to hold your fork the right way?"

Many times. Many, many times. With most children, if there is something that you want done on a regular basis, you must nag on an ongoing basis. If Melanie's father wants her to hold her fork the right way, while Melanie strongly prefers the wrong way, he will have to say it meal after meal after meal. But if he persists, Melanie will gradually switch over to proper fork holding. It may take a long time but she will switch considerably sooner than if he says nothing.

But persistent nagging takes time and energy. Mary Alice and I wanted Nick and Margaret to learn a musical instrument. They both took piano lessons, but neither stayed with it although we encouraged them not to quit. "You will regret quitting once you are older. I know I did." (I had a baby self and a half, and I lasted all of one piano lesson.)

What You Can Do

A couple we know of had four children, all of whom became accomplished musicians. How did they succeed where we failed? How did the parents get all four of their kids to keep playing? Yes, it was a musical family and music appreciation ran in the family. Yes, being a musician was given a special respect within the family. But also, yes, the parents put a lot of time and energy in getting their kids to stay with it. Nobody is born loving to practice an instrument. Those parents really persisted, far more than Mary Alice and I did. We cared. We persisted. We nagged. But obviously it was not enough.

The same suggestion goes for good table manners, regularly putting clothes in the laundry, turning out lights when leaving a room, and a million other things you want your children to do or learn. If parents really care, their children will have good table manners and regularly put their clothes in the laundry. If they do not care quite enough, their children will not. How much you care and consequently how much energy you are willing to put in makes a huge difference. And again, as with so much of child raising, you have to pick and choose because you cannot accomplish everything. But what one expects and demands of children through their childhood is *not* a waste, even if it may seem to be. Our instructions to them over the years are lodged soundly in their heads.

For thirteen years, from age four to age seventeen, Nigel left his dirty clothes on the floor of his room. But then one day his father couldn't find Nigel's dirty clothes.

"Nigel, where are your dirty clothes?"

"In the laundry hamper."

"They are?"

"Yeah. What's the big deal? That's where they are supposed to go, right?"

"But Nigel, you have never done it before in your life."

"So?"

From that day on Nigel almost always put his dirty clothes in the hamper. What happened? Why was he finally doing it? Because he had always been told to and consequently knew and genuinely believed that he should. It was just that only now—at age seventeen—was he finally mature enough.

Business Parent

But nagging—continually repeating a demand—goes against your "say it once" advice. More important, it would only seem to play into the hands of the baby self who feeds on parental response. You keep telling us that the more of that it gets, the more it wants to stay around. How can nagging possibly work?

There is a trick to nagging. What the baby self feeds on is parent response. But in order for that response to be tasty to the baby self, it must have some emotion to it. The baby self wants feelings: anger, pleading, frustration, puzzlement, anything.

But what the baby self does not find tasty at all is a cold robotlike parent.

> *"Justin, I want you to pick up your room now."*
> *"I will. I promise. Later."*
> *"Justin, I want you to pick up your room now."*
> *"Why? It's not messy."*
> *"Justin, I want you to pick up your room now."*
> *"You always make me do stuff. I never get to have fun. I never do."*
> *"Justin, I want you to pick up your room now."*

Unflappable. Implacable. Cold. Unemotional. Calm. Not tasty at all. The mortal enemy of the baby self. *Business Parent.* With Business Parent, there is nothing for the baby self to grab hold of. Nothing for it to eat. The baby self hates Business Parent.

Business Parent is not like a parent at all. It is more like an absence of parent—replaced by a robot who will not go away until the room gets picked up. Business Parent is a worthy foe of the baby self.

A Secret Weapon: Nonresponse

Business Parent does not always get its way but usually it will prevail because it has developed the secret weapon of *nonresponse*—that is, nonresponse to the baby self.

A few years ago I observed this scene in a bank.

A two-year-old girl was happily writing on deposit slips while her mother waited in line. Finished with her banking, the mother picked up her daughter and started toward the exit. Immediately her daughter burst into tears. She didn't want to leave the deposit slips. The girl's mother did nothing in regard to the crying. She simply continued to walk to the bank's exit, carrying her sobbing daughter. As they got to the door, the girl turned her head to look at what was going on outside the bank. She stopped crying. She asked her mother a question that I could not hear. They then left the bank and went out into the street. The little girl was no longer crying.

Nonresponse is such an especially useful tool in child raising because of its effect on the less desirable aspects of the baby self. It is in many situations the one and only kind of response that can achieve positive results. However, the effective use of nonresponse is something of an art. But once perfected, its effect is nothing short of miraculous.

At its best the art of nonresponse does not ignore the child, only the child's undesirable behavior. The secret to this art is to continue the normal flow of what would go on as if the undesirable behavior were simply not happening. It's especially effective with some of the most unpleasant child behaviors, such as sulking, whining, and temper tantrums—subjects I will specifically address in Chapter Four.

In this chapter, I want to give you a sampling of how the art of nonresponse can be used in diverse encounters with the baby self. Each encounter depicts two kinds of parental response, one that engages the baby self in the child and one that does not. If you read these out loud, you can actually feel the difference.

Engaging

"This stew is too salty. I can't eat it."

"Well, dear, it's what's for supper."

"But I can't eat it."

"Well, that's what's for supper."

"But I can't eat this supper. I want something else."

"I'm not going to make you something else. You're going to have to learn to eat some things you don't like."

"But I can't eat this. It's too salty. It makes me want to throw up. I want something else."

"I'm not going to make you something else."

"But I'll be hungry. I hate this stew."

Not Engaging

"This stew is too salty. I can't eat it."

"I'm sorry you don't like the stew, dear."

"But I can't eat it."

"Gosh, I guess you won't eat the stew then."

"But I want something else. I can't eat this."

"Well, if you find something else—of course, not snack food—that's fine, dear."

"But there is nothing else. You make me something."

"Gosh, I guess you're stuck with a bad meal."

"But I can't eat this. I hate it."

"Gosh, I guess then you'll be hungry."

Engaging

"Mom, J.J. keeps drooling."

"Stop drooling, J.J."

"I'm not drooling. Carla's lying."

"He is drooling. Look."

"J.J., stop teasing your sister."

"I'm not doing anything. She's a liar."

"I'm not. He was drooling."

Not Engaging

"Mom, J.J. keeps drooling."

"Oh."

"Make him stop."

Silence.

"Make him stop."

Silence.

"I'm going to drool on him back."

More silence.

Engaging

"Mom, I don't know where my shoes are."

"Did you look for them?"

"Yeah. I can't find them."

"Well, where was the last place you left them?"

"I don't know. I don't remember. I don't know where they are."

"Jeremy, we have to leave in ten minutes. Now go and try to find your shoes."

"I don't know where they are."

"Jeremy, I have really had it with you. We have to go in ten minutes and now I am going to have to hunt for your shoes."

"I don't know where they are."

"I'm going to glue your shoes on you."

"No, that would hurt."

"I'm only kidding, Jeremy."

"That would hurt."

Not Engaging

"Mom, I don't know where my shoes are."

"Oh, you can't find your shoes."

"I don't know where they are."

"Gosh, that's a problem. We'll be going soon."

"I can't find them."

"Well, I sure hope you find them before it's time to go."

Engaging
  "Mom!"

"What, dear?"

"Why is this finger longer than the other one?"

"That's just the way you're made."

"But why is it longer?"

"It just is. I don't know dear. Everybody's like that. See, mine is too."

"But why is it?"

"What do you think, dear?"

"I don't know why. That's why I'm asking you. Why?"

"I don't know, dear. That's just the way people are made."

"But why? Look, it's shorter than the other."

"Vinnie, I don't know what to say to you. It just is."

"But why?"

"I don't know, dear. Maybe it makes it better for using all your fingers."

"I don't understand. What do you mean it makes it better for using my fingers?"

"Vinnie, this is getting very aggravating."

"I just want to know."

Not Engaging
  "Mom!"

"What, dear?"

"Why is this finger longer than the other one?"

"That's just the way you're made."

"But why is it longer?"

"It just is. I don't know dear. Everybody's like that. See, mine is too."

"But why is it?"

"I really don't know, dear."

"But why do you think it is?"

"I just don't know."

Silence. Vinnie walks away.

Engaging
"Mom, Becky ate some of the pastries that were supposed to be for the party."

"Becky! Come here."

And then their mother gets into it with Becky. (While her sister's baby self says, *"ALL RIGHT!"*)

Not Engaging
"Mom, Becky ate some of the pastries that were supposed to be for the party."

Forbidden knowledge. Unless dangerous to self or others, it is inadmissible evidence against Becky, even if true.

"Oh, that's too bad."

"She ate the pastries. You said we weren't supposed to."

"That's right."

"Well, Becky ate some of the pastries."

"Yeah, she wasn't supposed to."

"*Aren't you going to do something?*"

"*I hope she doesn't eat any more. I hope you don't eat any of them.*"

"*But I didn't. Becky did.*"

"*Oh, that's too bad.*"

"*But she wasn't supposed to.*"

"*Yeah.*"

Engaging

"*Eduardo, I told you not to use my tools.*"

"*I didn't. Maria did.*"

"*Eduardo, don't lie to me.*"

"*I didn't. Maria used them. Why do you always say it's me?*"

"*Because it is always you, Eduardo. Maria never uses the tools.*"

"*Yes, she does.*"

"*Eduardo, stop lying.*"

"*I'm not lying. I didn't use the tools. I don't know who did.*"

"*Eduardo, do you want to go to your room until you can figure out who used the tools?*"

"*I didn't use them. It's not always me. I'm not lying. I'm not.*"

Not Engaging

"*Eduardo, I told you not to use my tools.*"

"*I didn't. Maria did.*"

"*Eduardo, do not use my tools.*"

"But I didn't. Maria did. Why do you always say it's me?"

"I do not want you to use my tools again."

"I didn't."

"You heard me, Eduardo."

And Eduardo's father exits.

BJ and Cheryl got two different toys in their fun boxes at Burger Boy.

Engaging
"Cheryl's toy is better than mine and she won't trade. It's not fair."

"I'm sorry you don't like your toy, BJ."

"But it's not fair. Her toy is better."

"Well, we can't go and buy a whole other fun box."

"But it's not fair."

"Well, sometimes things aren't the way you want them."

"But it's not fair. She got a better toy."

"But everything isn't always fair, BJ. You have to learn that. Other times you get better than her. Maybe next time."

"No, I never will. It's not fair. I want her toy."

"Well, you can't have hers, BJ. You're just going to have to be satisfied with yours."

"But I'm not. I hate mine. I hate it." BJ throws his toy on the floor.

"BJ, if it breaks you won't get another one."

"I don't care. I hate mine."

Not Engaging
   "Cheryl's toy is better than mine and she won't trade. It's not fair."

   "Gosh, that's too bad."

   "But it's not fair. Her toy is better."

   "Yeah, it would make me mad too."

   "But I want a different one. It's not fair."

   "I don't know what to say, dear."

   "You have to get me a different one."

   "You sure don't like your toy."

   "It's not fair. I want a different one."

   Silence.

   BJ stares grumpily at his sister's toy, but says no more.
   The best way to characterize the overall differences between these two kinds of parental responses might be that the one that tends to engage the baby self has a feeling of moving *toward* one's children, wanting to grab hold of them and do something with them. The responses that do not engage the baby self seem to let go, or mildly deflect. You could think of it as different ways of responding to a big beach ball being thrown at you. You can catch it, squeeze it, examine it, and poke at it. Or you can just let it hit you wherever it does and bounce off, paying it no mind, going on about your business. Or each time the ball comes to you, you can gently tap it back, not catching it, just gently tapping back. With the dialogues that unintentionally engage the baby self, the child has something to play off of and build on emotionally. But with the dialogues that do not, the parent's response deflates the

potential emotional feeding of the baby self and the child can't get much going. One way builds, the other deflates. If you can learn to use it, the art of not responding to the baby self may become your most reliable and most called-upon parenting strategy.

Your Own Self-Restraint

One problem with nonresponse is that sometimes it is hard to do. It can go against many of our natural tendencies that often lead us to say more, do more, than what is perhaps best. That is, part of the art of effective parenting involves self-restraint. A good example of this is with listening. To be a good listener definitely involves both skill *and* self-restraint.

Good Listening

We have talked about times not to listen, but there are many more times when parents need to listen to their children and do *nothing* more than listen. Listening is a very special part of child raising. What is so especially good about listening is that it gives children a chance to fill the room with themselves, what they think, care about, their opinions, their stories. Being heard makes them feel important and is an extremely self-affirming process.

The art of listening is in staying with what they are saying and *not* taking what they are saying in some other direction even if we feel it might be helpful. Carl Rogers, an influential psychotherapist of the 1950s and '60s, was a master of good listening. When he responded to his clients, he would repeat to them a shortened, sometimes slightly altered, but often exact version of what they had just said. A typical dialogue would be:

"I went to the store and I had a terrible time. I couldn't find anything I wanted."

"You had a terrible time at the store. You couldn't find anything you wanted."

"That's right. It doesn't seem like it's worth going out sometimes. You never accomplish anything."

"You feel that sometimes going out is a waste of time, as you don't accomplish anything."

"You said it. It gets so depressing some of the time."

"You feel it gets very depressing sometimes."

"Yeah it does. Like last Thursday with Harold . . ."

I once saw a film of Carl Rogers with a client and he really did say back to her exactly what she had just said. It may seem stupid but the truth is, as any psychotherapist knows, that it's remarkably effective simply to allow people to say what they have to say. The result is very beneficial: They feel they have been heard.

Too often our parenting fervor can get in the way of good listening. Our innate parenting instincts get in the way of our children's chance to be onstage. Sometimes we want to be helpful when they don't need our help.

Carole Ann to her mother:

"Mom, I don't like Kristin Wuhlmeyer."
"Why, dear?"
"She's a jerk. She wouldn't give me a turn. She kept hogging the Whirlycycle."
"Did you ask her nicely?"
"Yeah. She just wouldn't. She's a hog."
"Well, maybe you just have to wait longer."
"She will never give it to me. She's a jerk."

"Well, it is her Whirlycycle. Maybe you have to wait until she stops for a while, and then tell her how you would really like to have a turn."

"She's a big pig. She will never give me a turn."

"Well, maybe she won't. Sometimes people just don't want to share no matter how much you ask."

"She's a pig."

"Sometimes you have to go off and find something to do on your own."

"Not with piggy Kristin Wuhlmeyer."

What Carole Ann's mother has said was all good and helpful. Her words were an appropriate model for her child's handling of a frustrating situation. But Carole Ann only wanted to tell her mother what a big pig Kristin Wuhlmeyer was. At the end of their conversation, Carole Ann was dissatisfied with the outcome.

"Mom doesn't understand what a big pig Kristin Wuhlmeyer is."

Better listening might have been:

"I don't like Kristin Wuhlmeyer."

"You don't?"

"No, she's a jerk."

"Why? What did she do?"

"She wouldn't give me a turn. She kept hogging the Whirlycycle."

"That was pretty selfish."

"Yeah, she's a big pig. I would like to sock her in the nose."

"You were mad."

"I would like to sock her in the nose twice. She is the biggest pig in the world."

"You were really mad."

"Yeah. What are we having for supper?"

Carole Ann was mad because Kristin Wuhlmeyer had hogged the Whirlycycle. She wanted to tell her mother about it and how mad she was at Kristin Wuhlmeyer. By telling her mother *her* story about Kristin, Carole Ann was able to present a part of herself, something that happened to her and what she thought about it. Having told this to her mother, Carole Ann had accomplished what she wanted, felt listened to, and had nothing more to say. Her mother had heard her story, understood it, and appreciated it. Carole Ann was happy.

In order to let this happen as parents, we must restrain ourselves and listen and listen only. Carole Ann was not looking to her mother to solve a problem because there was no problem to be solved. If there had been a problem, she would have said so. "How can I get Kristin Wuhlmeyer to let me play on her Whirlycycle?"

Survival Training

But there is much in child raising where nonresponse is not simply an art to make matters go more smoothly, it is a necessity. For we cannot always fill the rough spaces in our children's lives. In order for them to grow, to mature, much of that work *must* be done by them.

As our children grow, we *must* also leave space for them to learn to deal with whatever they encounter in their day-to-day lives. For real traumas, serious upsets, or disappointments, children need compassion and understanding. But for other upsets, the job of working through their bad feelings should be left to them to do on their own.

They can do it, but they definitely need practice. It is perhaps the early-childhood equivalent of the survival training in which they leave you on a deserted island with only a penknife and a book of matches and you're supposed to survive for a week. It is supposed to be good for you; it is supposed to give you confidence that you can survive on your own with nobody to lean on, no matter what. Children who are off by themselves go through a very definite and hugely important survival training. They learn—so long as their parents do not interfere and get in the way of the process—that emotionally they can survive on their own. They learn that they have the means within their own little bodies (from the nurturing that has already been laid down inside of them and is a part of them) to make the bad feelings go away. In a relatively short time, they can work through all their bad feelings wholly on their own. All they have to do is wait a little while and gradually it happens.

For children to learn this skill, parents will have to watch their children suffer. Parents do not want to do this because so often they are the cause of the suffering. Even with the mildest and most unassuming children, it is inevitable that there will be times when our wants and theirs will conflict, and we will be the cause of their suffering and make them have bad feelings. Somehow they have to learn to survive— at least for a while—without us.

> *"No, you cannot watch any more TV. That's it."*
> *"But it's not fair. Why can't I? Why?"*
> *"No, I don't want to hear any more about it."*
> *"But it's not fair. IT'S NOT FAIR."*
> *"Get out of here, Corey."*
> *"No, you're not fair. I hate you."*

A screaming Corey was subsequently deposited on his bed in his room. Even two rooms away, through a closed door and down a long corridor, Corey's mother could still hear him.

But then, if Corey's mother were to do nothing and leave him alone screaming in his room, a funny thing might happen.

> *"YOU'RE NOT FAIR. I HATE YOU. I DO."*

What You Can Do

I hate Mommy. I do. I hate Mommy. She's not fair. She never is. I hate her. I wish I had different parents. Not her. She's mean. She doesn't care about my feelings . . .

Nobody cares about my feelings. Only me cares about my feelings. Nobody cares about me. Nobody does. Nothing ever happens to me that's good. Only bad . . .

Bad things never happen to Billy Soloman. He gets everything he wants. He has a better bike than me. I wish I lived in his house . . .

No, I wish I lived in a palace. And I got everything, all for me. And I'd have a pet tiger. And he'd eat people I don't like. I wonder what tigers eat—besides people? I wonder if they eat cereal? I'm sort of hungry. But not for cereal. I wonder what's for supper.

"MOM, what's for supper?"

And quite possibly not fifteen minutes after a sobbing and furious Corey had been placed in his room—with no intervening action at all by his mother—he emerges in a totally good mood, as if nothing had happened.

It is hugely important that children learn this skill. To learn to deal with bad feelings on one's own is one of the foundations of mental health. Children who cannot are then stuck. They can never deal with disappointment, but must always carry situations on and on, seeking resolutions they can never get, unable to take a loss and move on. Or they become wholly dependent on others to deal with any such feelings. As teenagers and adults, they can become far more vulnerable to seeking whatever escapes life has to offer, which definitely includes drugs and drinking, to get rid of their bad feelings. Fortunately, most children usually develop this skill regardless of what their parents do.

Because of the great importance of children's experiencing and learning to deal with this situation—parent and child in direct opposition—I am wary of parents who always try to be comforting, always try to be understanding. A parent does not want to be too helpful in softening bad feelings, particularly when those feelings are a result of everyday confrontations. Parents must be careful. There are times when it is very definitely okay to be an ogre to one's children—when one's basic crime is going against what they want. Children have to learn to deal with bad feelings on their own. But for our children to accomplish this and so many other day-to-day living skills, we must let them practice, which means we must also let go.

The Ultimate Question

When Nick, our firstborn, came home from the hospital, he slept in a crib in our room for the first few days. But then we decided to have him sleep in what was to be his room, which was separated from ours by a short hallway. That night we put a sleeping Nick in his room and went to bed. This was a big step because we had not been separated from him except for very brief periods of time. Could he survive?

I remember getting up at maybe three or four in the morning to go in to get him for his feeding. He had been silent during the intervening four hours. My memory is that I did not go into his bedroom wondering, "Is he still alive?" I went in thinking, "I am going in there to get my dead son."

Newborns are fragile. When they are first entrusted fully to our care, they have not existed for very long. They are so close in time to their birth, we can't help but feel that they are potentially close to not being alive. And during our early care of them, we notice that when we are with them, watching over them, they seem able to stay alive.

That one time and subsequent instances of Nick's surviving alone in the other room for four hours while we slept did not convince me that I was wrong in anticipating his death because of the separation. But at least I began to entertain the possibility that Nick could actually—if mainly only by lucky chance—survive for significant chunks of time without me or his mother being right there with him.

It is an important issue, for it continues. Do we allow our child to be in the care of someone other than us? Do we trust our child in the care of people with whom he might not be familiar—baby-sitters? And as a child gets older, this under-lying question—can my child survive without me?—becomes one of the major issues of child raising. Can I allow my child to have parts of his or her life over which I have no control? Can I let him ride his bike around the block? (I remember watching Nick for the first time ride his bike out of sight and then submissively, quietly, waiting for the sirens, not won-dering *would* he get hit by a car.) Can I let him go over to a friend's house where I don't know that much about the parents? Can I let him be in his room alone when he is very angry? Can I trust him to be at the playground unsupervised and not go off with strange people? Can I trust that the world is not so dangerous, that he is not so vulnerable, that his judgment is not so poor, that I do not have to supervise, do not have to oversee everything? Will he ever possess the ability to survive on his own? Parenting requires faith—in ourselves and in our children.

We must have faith that if we have been good and loving parents, then they will have been nurtured enough. Despite the fact that the baby self—who wants when it does not always need—often makes it look just the opposite.

And we must have faith that though we do take chances—which we do—those chances are not so great but also are absolutely necessary.

The first part of parenting is nurturing. But the second part is letting go.

II

Classic Problems for
Parents and Children

4

Day In and Day Out

This section is about what happens every day—the actual situations that parents have to face. And it is here that the rules already discussed in these pages can have a major influence in making what goes on so much easier.

Whining, Sulking, and Temper Tantrums

We had a glimpse into the power of nonresponse in Chapter Three. However, nowhere in the realm of child raising is the power of nonresponse as clear and as absolute as in regard to those most beloved of child behaviors: whining, sulking, and temper tantrums. See for yourself.

Whining

"Mom, I can't button my sleeve," whines Darryl.

In response to whining there are basically three options:

(1) Respond as if they were speaking normally, not whining. *"Come here, Darryl. I'll see if I can help."*

(2) In some manner instruct the child not to whine.

"Stop whining! You know how I hate it when you whine."
"I am not going to listen to you when you whine."
"Say it without whining, and maybe I'll help."

Or—

(3) Absolutely ignore the whining as if the child were not speaking at all.

With responses 1 and 2, the whining will continue as part of a child's behavior. With response 3, if adhered to absolutely, always and without exception, children will not be whiners. The Whining Rule is that simple.

Nonresponse is so effective with whining because whining seems to come directly from the heart of the baby self. Since what the baby self eats for food is parents, if whining produces nothing, gets no notice from parents, it will wither and die. Any parent who has tried very hard but unsuccessfully to stop whining will truly appreciate the power of nonresponse.

Sulking

Robert wanted to go to McDonald's. Jennifer wanted to go to Burger King. The family went to Burger King. Throughout the meal at Burger King, Robert pouted. He said little and mainly sat turned around in his seat facing the booth behind him. Try as they might—alternately using threats and friendly words—his parents could not pull Robert out of his bad mood.

Nor did Robert stop when they left Burger King. He continued to sulk for a good hour once they had returned home. In fact, Robert continued to sulk until a favorite television show came on, at which time he simply dropped it.

The above, I think, is recognizable to most readers as a

classic sulk. Its aim, as with all sulks, is to provoke or keep going an intense emotional involvement with parents. An involvement which, as already discussed, is especially delicious—but not particularly nourishing—food for the baby self.

Incorrect responses to Robert's sulking would include:

1. Getting mad at him, lecturing him, threatening him.

"Stop that sulking, Robert, or I will give you something to sulk about."

"I am sick of you acting like a baby about everything. You don't get your way and you sulk. You are going to have to grow up."

These responses, as any parent of a sulker knows, would only intensify the sulking.

2. Trying to jolly Robert out of it.

"Come on, let's see a little smile. Come on now."

This is a direct challenge to the sulker to keep the sulk going. It only infuriates sulkers more. One may get a smile—sometimes the child cannot help it—but then sulkers will really redouble their efforts at sulking.

Or—

3. Trying to be understanding.

"What is it, Robert? I know you are mad. But sometimes you just can't get your way. And I know that makes you feel bad."

This response can in fact be a good response. Robert might respond:

"But it's not fair. Jennifer gets everything her way. You never do it my way. Always Jennifer. Never me."

And if Robert's parents were to allow Robert to rave, absolutely avoiding any attempts to respond, if they were to let Robert express his disappointment (it *is* disappointing going to Burger King when you wanted to go to McDonald's), and not get into an argument with him, Robert's disappointment might well dissipate and the sulk might end.

The only problem with being understanding is that it might not work. Robert might rave and then continue his sulk anyway. Or, as often is the case with professional sulkers, he would not want to be talked out of the sulk, no matter how understanding you are. He would want to keep the sulk going, and he would.

If parents want to be understanding with a sulker, they must also be ready not to invest too much in their efforts to end the sulk should this strategy fail. They must not hold it against the sulker that their attempts to be nice parents produced such poor results.

Some parents try to ignore sulkers, but not responding to the baby self and ignoring a child are not the same, and ignoring a sulking child is not a useful tactic. You can see this clearly when some parents choose to ignore the sulker as a counterattack, as retaliation for the sulking.

"Well, two can play this game. You're going to sulk. Okay, see how it feels for me to ignore you." (Not necessarily said out loud.)

This does not work. All it does is get into an emotional battle with the sulker, which is exactly what a parent does not want. All the other previous responses have a similar problem. They give the sulker something to respond to. Since the sulker's sole aim is to keep the emotional interaction going—"I want to make them feel bad. I want to make them beg me for forgiveness"—all the previous responses also provide potential ammunition. In fact, any response directed at the sulking allows the sulker to sulk in response. So what should parents do?

In response to Robert's sulking at Burger King, his parents should do nothing. They should allow him to sulk. They should act toward him as the beloved child he is who happens to be in a bad mood and is choosing not to talk.

"Robert, did you like seeing Aunt Martha? You hadn't seen her in a while."

Sulk.

"I did. I had a good time."
"Robert, would you hand me that pepper shaker?"

Sulk.

"Well, I guess I'll have to reach over and get it myself."
"Robert, do you remember if you turned off the TV before we left for Aunt Martha's?"

Sulk.

"Well, we'll find out when we get home."
"Robert, can you see the clock from where you are sitting?"

Sulk.

"Oh, I can see it if I lean over."

If you need a response from the sulker, do not force it. Instead, make a decision based on your best guess as to what he probably would decide. He always has the ongoing option of voicing his opinion if he so chooses.

"What would you like to eat, Robert?"

Sulk.

"Well, I'll get you a Whopper with cheese, a small fries, and a medium Coke. Is that okay? Let me know if you want something different."

Rather than:

"What would you like, Robert?"

Sulk.

"Well then, I guess you don't want anything."

You might get a response, "I want a Whopper with cheese," but you might not. The battle would continue and Robert would be angry at his parents for forcing him to say something when he did not want to. What parents want to do is to allow the sulker to sulk, and then continue on as they would anyway.

They want to say to the sulker:

"You can sulk as long as you want. It is totally okay with me. I still love you as I always do. I am not going to try to get you out of it, but I am not going to pay any special attention to you either. But if you want it in any way to disrupt the flow of what is going on, that simply is not going to happen."

In effect, our behavior wants to say:

"You may be in a bad mood, but I'm not. Rather than respond to your bad mood, I am going to continue being in my good mood. If you want to sulk, that's fine. I will go about my normal business, which includes that I love you a lot."

Temper Tantrums

On a Saturday morning, Alex's father was taking dirty clothes out of Alex's room to put in the wash.

"No, don't take my doggy shirt. I want to wear my doggy shirt today."

"I'm sorry, Alex, it needs to be washed."

"But I want to wear my doggy shirt."

"I'm sorry, Alex. It needs washing and I'm doing the laundry this morning. You will have to wear something else."

Alex's father proceeded to carry the armful of dirty clothes out of Alex's room to where he was collecting the laundry that needed to be taken to the laundromat. Alex followed his father.

"Don't take my doggy shirt! I want to wear my doggy shirt!"

Alex began trying to pull the doggy shirt out from the bundle that his father was carrying.

"No, Alex," said Alex's father, lifting the clothes out of Alex's reach. "You can't have the doggy shirt. It needs to be washed."

Alex then began simultaneously pushing his father and screaming, "I want my doggy shirt! I want it!"

"No, Alex!"

Alex started to cry and kick.

"I want my doggy shirt! I want my doggy shirt!"

This is what is known as a temper tantrum. Temper tantrums are a child's way of saying, "I am not getting my way, I am not happy about it, and I want that changed now!"

When you think about it, the fact that a child is throwing a tantrum is not necessarily a bad sign at all. Temper tantrums are usually an indication that parents have done their job. They have appropriately set a limit and, consequently but not intentionally, frustrated their child. The temper tantrum is their child's recognition of that limit and his displeasure with it.

What Not to Do about Temper Tantrums

Parents need to be extremely wary that by their reactions to temper tantrums they do not change a victory into a loss. Parents seriously err when they try to stop a tantrum, because their efforts all too easily end up merely feeding the baby self, and rather than stopping the tantrum, they make it worse and more certain to recur. Mistaken attempts to stop tantrums can take a number of forms:

1. Giving in right away.

This is acceptable only—as previously discussed—where the specific situation or one's own not-up-to-it mood makes swift capitulation strategically wise. But a parent must not allow on a regular basis for tantrums or threats of tantrums to bully them into changing their mind.

"I'll let him stay up another half an hour. He always has such a fit if I don't."

2. Anger or threats.

"You just better cut that out now or you're in big trouble."

Anger and threats are the *worst* response to a tantrum. They answer anger with more of the same, and will only fuel a tantrum. Tantrum throwers may not have gotten their parents to change their mind, but they certainly got a major reaction. The tantrum *was* a success. Consequently, tantrums will continue and they will be big.

3. Reasoning.

"Now, Alex, a temper tantrum is not going to get you anything. I'm not going to change my mind. You always have liked your fish shirt, and it's clean. You'll see, it will be just as much fun to wear."

This is fine as a response, but often it will not work. As you know by now, the baby self is far less interested in solutions than it is in keeping arguments going.

"But I hate my fish shirt."

"But you've always said you liked your fish shirt."

"I don't. I hate it. I want my doggy shirt."

"Listen, Alex, you can have your doggy shirt as soon as I finish doing the wash this afternoon."

"I want my doggy shirt now."

"But, Alex, it's very dirty."
"I don't care. I want my doggy shirt."

On and on he will go as long as he keeps getting parent response. This tantrum has succeeded, and he's primed for many more.

4. Affection.
"Come here, honey, do you want a hug?"
Actually, this is an excellent response. Sometimes a tantrum thrower, especially when tired, will respond to a hug, using the loving contact to calm himself down. But showing affection has its limits, because hugs are often not what tantrum throwers want. Hence, hugs should be offered on an "if you want it, it is here" basis, with parents understanding that it may be rejected and that is okay too.

But doesn't a hug feed the baby self, and therefore reward the tantrum?

It probably does, but apparently in a good way. For clearly, in practice, hugs, when accepted, speak to the part of the baby self that *needs* affection, that *is* truly nurtured, and not to the part that wants everything but does not need it.

5. Understanding.
"I know you're disappointed, honey. You really want to wear your doggy shirt today. You're sad and you're mad that you can't wear it. But you can wear it lots and lots of other times."

This also is an excellent response. Alex knows that he is being heard and often that is all he wants and all he needs. The tantrum is over.

"I did. I did. I wanted to wear my doggy shirt. I love my doggy shirt. I do. It's my favorite. Is my fish shirt clean?"

But often this will not work. Understanding is like affection: It should only be offered to a tantruming child because it is always a nice thing to give to a child, but again parents should be aware that it might not work.

6. An exception to the rule—physical restraint.

"No, Jimmy, I am not going to let you kick me." And Jimmy should be removed—if possible—or held until he stops trying to kick. (Obviously, with older and bigger children, this becomes a whole other and much tougher problem.) Again, parents should not actively try to stop tantrums, only their potentially harmful parts.

What to Do about Temper Tantrums

Tantrums may be healthy and necessary but they are also unpleasant to be around. Since temper tantrums need to be made as ineffective as possible, the best response to tantrums is to ignore them. But often tantrums are simply too unpleasant or go on too long to ignore. In which case banishment to elsewhere—separation—until the tantrum is over becomes the appropriate response. A good rule is that as soon as you *start* to feel aggravated by a tantrum, put distance between yourself and your tantrum thrower. This often means picking up tantrum throwers and carrying them to their room, to another room, or to a time-out place. If a parent does this quickly and regularly, children often go on their own without having to be carried, knowing that if they do not they *will* be carried.

"*Good-bye, Kevin,*" and Kevin himself, still screaming, exits to his room, knowing if he does not, he will immediately be carried there. This is an important parental bottom line: If a temper tantrum is too unpleasant to ignore, separation between child and parent will be an early and inevitable result. The separation will occur voluntarily or involuntarily.

But the banishment is not a punishment; as soon as the tantrum is over, tantrum throwers are welcome to return. If they return and continue fussing, they are banished again until the tantrum is truly over. In effect, the parent says, "You *can* have a tantrum, but not around me."

The wise parent also wants to say, "You can have tantrums, but they are not going to accomplish anything. I'm not going to change my mind or give you a lot of extra attention. On the other hand, I will not hold the tantrum against you. When you have a tantrum, you gain nothing and you lose nothing."

If tantrums are continually rendered ineffective, they will be resorted to less, and their overall frequency, duration, and intensity will definitely be reduced. However, tantrums will not disappear altogether because they are too much a part of being a child.

When Children Are Angry at Their Parents

"I Hate You"

Tara, to her mother:

"I hate you and I hate Daddy, and I hate this house and I hate everybody. And I'm not kidding. I don't want to live here anymore."

"Get out of here and up to your room before I carry you there."

"I hate you."

Tara, alone in her room, may think some very angry thoughts about her mother. "She is the meanest mommy in the world. I hate her. I'd like to smack her real hard in the face, and maybe she would get a bloody nose. I wish she wasn't my mother. I'll bet she's not. I'll bet I have a *real* mother, and I'll bet she would never treat me this way."

Yet if time goes on and Tara's mother leaves her alone, gradually the anger goes away, to the point where Tara is no longer angry at her mother at all. But even though her anger has dissipated, Tara worries about the consequences of her anger.

Is everything all better and back to normal? Has something bad happened because I was so mad at Mommy?

Children *do* worry like this. They fear the consequences of their own anger.

I really did feel like smashing Mommy in the face. Is Mommy okay?

Or maybe worse still, Tara worries that her mother might reject her because of her angry words.

"You say you hate me, Tara? Then I don't think you have to live here anymore. You like Becky's mother better? Then you can live with her from now on. I'm going to call Mrs. Porter right now."

These are not minor issues. Children must feel that their anger toward their parents is not a dangerous thing. They can get angry at their parents and yet, because they are so little and their attachment to their parents so secure, nothing bad will result. This is a useful and reassuring lesson. It reinforces that they and their anger are part of the little world of childhood and cannot seriously threaten the big adult world of Mommy and Daddy on which they so totally depend. The alternative is just too scary.

I mean I'm only a little kid. Sometimes I wish I lived some-where else, but not really. I want my Mommy and Daddy. What would I do if I didn't have them?

It is equally important that parents understand that children's anger is no big deal. But "I hate you. I don't want to live here anymore" are nasty words. And if parents take them at all to heart it can make them feel lonely, rejected, and out of grace with their child. And though one may realize that it will only be for a while, it still hurts. Parents might be compelled to try to fix the situation because the words sting too much and because they want to return to their normal warm and cozy relationship, back to "Mommy loves you and you love Mommy." Tara's mother might go into Tara's room and attempt a reconciliation.

"Are you still mad at me, Tara? You know I love you. You know I don't want to make you feel bad."

But when her mother tries to fix things, Tara learns that her anger is unsettling to her mother, that it's powerful and hence scary. Her baby self learns that this is an excellent means to manipulate her mother. None of the above helps Tara or her mother.

But maybe Tara does mean what she says. I do everything for Tara. All I care about is that she's happy. How could she possibly say all that to me? Does Tara want to live somewhere else? Even a little?

"No, of course I don't hate Mommy. I just get mad at her sometimes. Because sometimes she's mean to me. But I love her. I don't want anybody else. Mommy knows that when I say stuff it's just because I'm mad. Mommy knows that. *Doesn't she?"*

If you are in the role of major caregiver, your child's deep true attachment is to you and none other. It is a mistake to forget that. It is you that she loves—and always will.

We make a big mistake if we take their mean comments personally. Comments, for example, that might hurt our feelings truly and justifiably were they said to us by an adult. But they are not adults. They are children, our children, who, not fearing us and secure in our love when angry at us, say what they feel like. But not necessarily at all what they truly deeply mean. Which often only a short time later they will tell us.

"I don't hate you, Mommy. I do love you. Do you still love me?"

"You Don't Love Me"

"You don't love me," sobbed Winston at the entrance to the family room, literally slobbering as the tears poured down.

"How can you say that?" said his father. "You know I do."

"You don't love me," again sobbed Winston, choking as he cried.

The vast majority—if not all—of children say the above *precisely* because they do know that their parents love them. They say it, knowing the love and having learned that saying "You don't love me" upsets their parents. And at that particular moment that is exactly what they want to do—because they are angry.

The particular irony of "You don't love me" is that children who actually seriously at some level might think that their parents may not love them would *never* say it. The actual thought in a child's mind that their parents might not love them is much too devastating, too terrifying, to ever bring up directly.

Hence, "You don't love me" really means:

"I know you love me, which is why I'm saying the opposite because I know it will upset you which is what I want to do because I'm mad at you."

Children say all kinds of things when they are upset with their parents. But that does not mean that the words are true. If parents are genuinely concerned by their child's words, they should ask—at a neutral time. But the fact remains that children—not unlike us—at any given time may say how they feel then, which may not at all be how they—or we—actually feel overall.

Bedtime

What's that noise? It sounds like somebody's there. Mommy says it's the "house settling." I don't even know what that means. I mean I know that there really isn't anybody there. Not a robber, not monsters.

I wonder if Grandpa who died before I was born can watch me?

I wonder if his ghost would ever come back? In my room? Like now. When it's dark?

I wonder if Suzy Kramer is going to tease me tomorrow. I hate it when she teases me. I wish she was dead. No, I don't wish she was dead. It's bad to wish that somebody is dead. Uh oh, now maybe something bad is going to happen to me.

I'm never going to get to sleep now. I wish Mommy was here. Did something just move?

"Mom! I'm thirsty."

Bedtime is the number-one time in a child's life for being alone and therefore becomes a major time of separating from parents. Bedtime, a time of vulnerability, worries, and no parents, is anathema to the baby self. *I think I'd rather not.*

"Mom, read to me some more."
"Dad, my tooth hurts."

Bedtime is leaving the safety of parents to drop off into the unknown of infinite terrors.

"And if I die before I wake I pray the Lord my soul to take."
If I die?
"Mommy. My nose is stuffy."

But though the separation at bedtime is loathed by the baby self, that same separation is important for parents. For many parents, the only time they get to be by themselves or to do what they feel like doing is after their children are in bed. It can be *their* only baby-self time. Parents deserve that time and need it. A child's intrusion into that time can be very hard on parents.

"How many times do I have to tell you to get into your pajamas? It is way past your bedtime. We will talk in the morning about whether you can get a rabbit."

It is useful to have a set bedtime, although one can be flexible.

"Can't I stay up to watch *Grown-Up Kids* this one time?"
"Sure."

But more important, parents do need to be firm about bedtime. That is, once bedtime arrives, that's it.

But what is bedtime?

What kind of question is that? Bedtime is when my kids are in bed with the lights out and maybe the night light is on and talking is over.

This is one possible definition of bedtime. But the secret of easy bedtimes uses a different definition of bedtime. *Bedtime is the end of interaction with parents.* Bedtime is when nurturing parents leave for good until tomorrow morning and all that is left are the robotlike Business Parents.

"Go to bed, Stephen."
"But I can't sleep. I keep thinking about snakes."
"Go to bed, Stephen."

And if they call, don't answer.

"Mom. Mom. Mom. Mom. Mom. Mom."

And if one does not go to them or answer, they will stop.

But what if . . .

If it really is something important—they are genuinely sick, there is actual blood, there *is* smoke in their room—you will know.

Otherwise, their pleas are simply the baby self not wanting to separate.

"Dad. Dad. I can't find Teddy Gray."

And if they get up, send them back to bed.

"Go to bed, Stephen."

If they have to go to the bathroom, they can go. Why do they have to get permission?

"Mom. Mom. Mom. I have to go to the bathroom."

And if they are little and they get up, quickly put them back in bed.

"Hi," says four-year-old Jeffrey, wandering in.

"Go to bed, Jeffrey."

"I don't want to go to bed."

That early in the sequence, Jeffrey's parents should pick him up and put him back in bed. If children are too old to carry, or might put up a fight, tell them to go to bed. Waste no more words than:

"Go to bed, Stephen."

If he does not, treat him as persona non grata. Give him no more recognition than a piece of furniture. Don't yell at him, discuss anything with him, or lecture him. Staying up past bedtime will lose its appeal for children if interaction with their parents turns into interaction with a friendly but unresponsive thing that only looks like a parent. They will do it less.

"Go to bed, Irina."
"But it's too itchy."
"Go to bed, Irina.

Not—

"There's sand in my bed. It's too itchy."
"Well, brush it off."

They can figure that out themselves.

To some parents the above might sound a little harsh. They feel their children might need them in order to get through that alone time, that transition, until they are safely in the arms of sleep. But this is one of those times when children, if they have enough good nurturing, can work things out on their own. They will have internalized the sense of "I'm okay" that can sustain them for just such times and, if they need to, they can transfer it to Teddy, blanky, Mr. Huggles, or their thumb until they fall asleep.

Children do need their parents at night. They need them at hand, available, and always watching over them. But they do not need them right there, with them and talking to them. Once in bed with "goodnights" over, perhaps what children need of Mom and Dad is like the moon. It's up there, always watchful, friendly, but not doing a whole lot.

But that does not stop them from wanting more.

"Daddy. Daddy. I think there's a bug in my bed."

Saying Good Night

How much of sitting with them, story reading, saying good night, is appropriate? As long as you enjoy doing it, as much as you want. But once you decide it is over and now it is bedtime—the designated time of child and parent separation—interaction needs to be over until morning.

" 'And then Bunny Hopkins put away his gardening tools and came inside. Would the candy he planted start sprouting tomorrow? He hoped so.' Good night, my darling darlingest."

"Please, Mommy, just a little more. Just a little?"
"Good night, my darling darlingest."

And exit.

The usual four hugs have just been given.

"Please, one more hug."
"Good night, Jessie." And exit.
"One more. Please. Just tonight."

But what if children do not go to sleep but instead stay up? What if they turn the light on? What if they are out of bed and playing?

If bedtime is defined as the end of interaction with parents, then that is what parents must stay with. "Evelyn, turn out the light and get in bed" is parental interaction. Obviously, Evelyn can get much of that if she keeps turning the light back on or getting out of bed. Parents must choose what bedtime means.

If children are playing loudly, yes, parents need to intervene. Or, if the TV is on in their room, and one wants to prohibit TV watching after bedtime, then certainly: "If you watch TV after bedtime, the TV comes out of your room." Or, if talking between brothers in the same room can be heard outside their room, "Quiet down, you two."

In reality some children do seem to need less sleep than others. What is so bad about letting those children play quietly in their room until they get sleepy and go to bed on their own, as long as they are not bothering anyone?

Children in Bed with Parents

If by necessity—limited space—parent and child must share the same bed, there is no problem. But there may be problems where the sharing of the bed is *in order to help a child go to sleep.* It just isn't necessary.

Children like to have their parents go to sleep with them so they don't have to lie in bed awake and alone. But parents can err by depriving their child of the chance to learn to deal with such times.

Tonight those monsters will eat me. I can smell them. Waiting until I am asleep. It will be tonight . . .

The great thing about monsters under the bed is that they do not exist. The fact that night after night the dreaded monsters never do come becomes very powerful reassurance—the best, in fact—that nothing happens when children are in bed alone.

I can survive. All on my own.

But if a parent intentionally provides that bridge by being in the same bed with the child until he or she falls asleep, where can the child ever learn to do it alone? Having never faced the bogeyman without a parent, he does not learn that he can.

Getting Up and Out in the Morning

"I can't stand it. By seven fifty when I finally get the kids out the door, I'm a nervous wreck. And I usually feel so guilty. There is so much fussing in the morning that they always go off to school in a bad mood."

"You don't know, my son Robby has made dawdling into an art form. I keep coming into his room, and, if possible, he is more undressed each time. Lying on the floor playing with his stupid cars. Not as if we have to be out of the house in ten minutes. He's like on the moon."

"With my daughter Geraldine, every morning is a scream-

*athon. She has a fit over everything. She can't find her un-
derpants. Her shirt has a spot on it. Her toast is too dark. By
the time she leaves, I want to strangle her."*

Getting up and out, actually leaving in the morning, goes
directly against all that the baby self stands for, and it wants
none of it. Mornings are not its favorite times because they
require a switch from the baby self to the mature self, which
the baby self never wants to allow. Children will do all they
can to dawdle and cling to Mommy or Daddy. The baby self
will invent endless problems and complaints, and will argue
over anything and everything.

"But why can't I bring my basketball to school?"

For parents, mornings come down to a choice between being
active participants in the entire process of their children's getting ready to go out.

*"Come on now, Sybil. Look at you. How are you going to
have time to eat?"*
*"Austin, where is your other shoe? You can't go to school
with only one shoe on. What did you do with your other shoe?"*

Or waiting, if that becomes necessary, until the very last
moment to enter the fray. Not only is the first way more
aggravating but it actually works against you. You are fighting
the baby self and are destined to lose.

My children trained me to handle mornings. They dem-
onstrated repeatedly that their progress in getting up and
dressed was *inversely* proportional to how much I got after
them. My presence, let alone my nagging—"Come on, Nicky,
get your shirt on"—absolutely seemed to inspire dawdling
rather than push them nearer to getting ready.

In the end I learned to be elsewhere, usually in the kitchen
fixing breakfast. Rather than go into their rooms, I would call

to them from a distance. (Where was Mary Alice? She says it was usually she, not I, who got them up and breakfasted.)

"Getting dressed?"
"Yeah."
"Ten minutes until we leave."
"You don't have to yell. I'm almost ready."

And they would usually get ready on time.

The secret of mornings is not to try very hard. You want to keep interaction—other than pleasant stuff that is not trying to accomplish anything—at an absolute minimum. In the morning, nagging just is not the way to go. All it accomplishes is that they still dawdle and argue and parents become infuriated. For dawdlers, even the most serious dawdlers, the ones who simply will not get ready, who can create real problems by making everybody else late, you have two choices: You can stand over them, badger them, threaten them, cajole them, every step of the way—which won't work. Or you can do something instead that does work.

1. Make sure they are awake and say, "Okay, time to get up and get dressed."
2. Periodically, cheerily call to them things like—"It's seven twenty-five."
   "You don't want to miss breakfast today, honeypumpkins. It's your favorite—waffles."
3. Do nothing else until ten minutes before it is time for them to leave. At which point, regardless of what stage they are in—even totally naked, lying on their backs on their beds counting spots on the ceiling—you call to them, "Five minutes!" (You are reserving an extra five minutes for Step 4.)
4. If the five minutes is up and they have failed to appear,

you go to where they are, and dress them very swiftly and not especially lovingly. (It's essential that you allow enough time at the end to avoid *everyone's* running late.) Get what they need for school, give them some kind of portable breakfast snack if they have failed to eat breakfast, and push them out the door. (It is a perfect place for Business Parent.)

In effect, this procedure says to children: You *can* dawdle the whole morning if you wish. But at the end, you will be dressed and out the door. You can have me do it my way at the end, or you can do it yourself. It's your choice.

Most children, given this choice, *will* usually dress themselves and get breakfast in the morning without any nagging from you. They'll probably still do it at the last minute, but they'll do it because they know that when you say "Five minutes" they have five minutes to either dress themselves or have you take over. More active efforts—riding them to move forward—clearly accomplish nothing.

"I'll Do It Later"

"Richard, would you please put the wet towels outside on the porch railing?"

"When I finish this," said Richard, who was busy sorting through his baseball cards.

"Richard, I asked you to put the towels out on the porch."

"I will," said Richard, who was now watching television. "As soon as this program's done."

"Richard, how many times do I have to tell you to take out the towels."

"You don't have to yell at me. I'm gonna do it," said Richard, still watching television, but definitely a different program.

"No, Richard. Now."

"Later" is not a very good idea unless we as parents are ready to accept the strong probability that later will not happen.

Mealtime

When I was a child, my family had sit-down-everybody-at-the-table meals every night. I remember them but not because I think they were an especially treasured part of my childhood (although, as a very fat little boy, I *was* exceptionally fond of the food). My main memory of those meals—besides the food—is that my older sister, Ellen, and I used that time to say nasty things to Mary, our younger sister. "Oh, I saw our sister today," I would comment offhandedly to Ellen, which always started Mary screaming. The point of my teasing was to imply that Mary, the only blonde in the family, was accidentally switched at the hospital and was not the natural child of our parents. No matter how many times we repeated this ploy, it was always a winner.

Mary Alice's and my working schedules often precluded nightly sit-down meals with our children. Most of our eating was done in front of the television, which I am personally very fond of. I'm not anyone to write of the sacredness of family meals. But clearly, with many families, it can be a special time shared and enjoyed by everyone. Meals together should not be an ordeal to get through.

At supper seven-year-old Lynnette kept up a stream of aggravating behavior.

"Why can't we ever have anything I like. Ooh, this is disgusting. Ooh, it's gross."

"If you don't like it, you don't have to eat it," said her mother.

"Keep your hands away from my plate," said Lynnette,

smacking her younger brother hard on his hand, which was nowhere near her at all.

"Don't hit Lyle. He wasn't doing anything," said her father. Whereupon Lynnette started kicking the underside of the table.

"Stop kicking the table," said her mother.

Whereupon Lynnette started rocking back in her chair. "Well, I hate my supper. I hate it. It's disgusting. Disgusting." She sort of whine-sang while she rocked.

Separation is in order if a given family member is making the meal significantly unpleasant for others. If someone is being obnoxious at meals, and seems intent on continuing to be obnoxious, there is no point in their being at the table. They are not harmed by eating elsewhere or at another time.

"Good-bye, Lynnette."

"No. I'm not doing anything."

"Good-bye, Lynnette."

If she is banished, remembering the rule for separation, she *is* welcome back at any time as long as she behaves. If family meals are a pleasant place to be, then the absented child will want to return—unless he or she is in a really bad mood or especially squirmy, in which case he or she might not want to return. In which case we wouldn't want them back either. Otherwise, not only will they tend to pull themselves together and want to return, but also they generally will learn to keep a little tighter cap on their behavior at meals.

Rules for Meals

1. Decide what level of meal chaos is acceptable to you.
2. Ignore what falls within acceptable limits of fussing or silliness. That means do not constantly correct. If you are going to have meals with human children, imperfect behavior will occur.

3. If a child is to the point where he or she is spoiling other people's mealtime, then the child should be banished quickly until he or she can return and be reasonably pleasant.

Family mealtimes are supposed to be pleasant times with or temporarily without a given family member.

"Good-bye, Edward."
"But I'm the father. I'm not supposed to be banished."
"Good-bye, Edward."
"Wait a minute. He didn't mean adults."
"Good-bye, Edward."
"Go for it, Mom."
"He didn't mean adults, Ruth."

Picky Eaters

"You said I could have dessert if I eat eight green beans. How about if I eat six?"
  "Eight."
  "Seven?"

He'll eat peanut butter and jelly sandwiches, sometimes carrot sticks, sometimes hot dogs, and that's it. And of course he'll eat any junk food.

All we as parents want is that each day our children get into their bodies an adequate amount of reasonably nutritious food. It's not asking a lot, but their eating can drive you crazy.

"Conrad, will you please stop playing with your food and eat."

"But I'm not hungry, and besides the skin on this piece of chicken is gross."

  "Well, I'll cut it off."

  "No. The gross skin has already touched the chicken."

But eating is the one area where we absolutely do not want to get into battles, because battles bring emotional issues into the realm of eating. We want eating to be emotion-free. We do not want to contaminate it with issues like control battles or love.

"Just eat those eight beans for me."
"It will make you happy?"
"Yes, it will make me happy."
"Then I won't."

So what should parents do? The main rule is do not try to *force* children to eat, either in general terms—"Come on, Simone. You have to eat something"—or specifically—"Eat the green beans."

In any given instance, forcing a child to eat might work. But overall, each time you try, it adds to the potential for future trouble. They will have learned that they can use eating as a means of entry into potential parent baiting, and they will.

The rules for meals need to be known and unequivocal before they ever sit down to a meal. There is no day-to-day negotiating, there is never anything to discuss.

For children who never seem to eat much, simply have meals and make the food available. Do *not* discuss their eating or not eating during the meal. If they just pick at their food instead of eating, limit mealtime. When mealtime is over, they can leave the table. Forget about their sitting at the table until they eat what you consider a sufficient amount.

Standard policy for picky eaters should include whether their food is still available to them after they leave the table, whether they are allowed to have an alternative (a peanut butter sandwich or cereal) if they want it, under what conditions they can have dessert, etc. It's your choice, and whatever policy you set is okay because it's your choice, it's standard policy, and there will never be any negotiating about it. However, making special and different meals is not a good policy. It only invites them to continue seeking special food treatment.

If you're worried about how much or how little they eat, ask their doctor if they are healthy. If they are healthy, how much of an eating problem can there be? If there is a problem, their doctor will let you know. Very few children living in homes where there is an adequate supply of food are under-nourished. The vast majority of children eat enough for their own nutritional purposes, especially if there is no emotional content to eating.

Acting Up in Public

Obnoxious at the Mall

Seven-year-old Brittany's family had a number of errands that they needed to do at the mall. But once there, Brittany began acting horribly. All attempts to improve her behavior failed.

When children continue to act up in public, deciding what to do and what not to do is relatively simple because there is not a whole lot you *can* do. Assuming that the more upbeat or reasonable methods have all failed, methods such as:

"Come on, Brittany, let's see which store has the prettiest decorations."

Or—

"Please, Brittany, we have a lot of errands we have to run. I know you don't want to be here, but it really would help me and Mom if you could try to not have tantrums."

Even—

"BRITTANY, YOU JUST BETTER SHUT UP!"

What is left?

When out in public with an obnoxious, fussing, demanding, or tantruming child with whom nothing seems to work, one should ride out the unpleasant time as best as one can. In effect, you have to tough it out.

You mean if my kid acts up when we're out in public, and if being nice, reasoning, and yelling all don't work (which of course they rarely do), *then there is nothing I can do? I just have to tough it out the whole rest of the time we're out?*

Yes. Not only is that all one should do but, as with temper tantrums, there are many things one should not do. Among them:

1. Reprimand the child for any length of time.

   "Brittany, why do you always have to have things your way? You are spoiling everything for all of us. You are going to have to learn that . . ."

   This is a reasonable and appropriate way to react, but as discussed repeatedly in this book, it will only engage the baby self and make matters worse than they already are.
2. Go home.

   This response seriously interferes with the rest of the family's plans. Going home is not fair to everybody else, it usually is very inconvenient, and it gives too much power to a child's fussing and tantruming. *My tantrums can control what we do. You'd better believe I'm going to keep having them.*
3. Offer rewards or bribes.

   "Now if you'll just control yourself and be good for the rest of the time, Daddy will buy you a treat."

   As discussed earlier, I do not like rewards, but I especially do not like them as means of quieting awful children. A promised reward may buy some quiet for any given time,

but I believe that in the long run it will accomplish nothing good.
4. Threaten punishment.

"If you don't behave, Brittany, you can forget about having Leslie over when we get back."

This is worse than promised rewards. Though it may work in any given instance, it will do nothing for the general improvement of out-in-public behavior. More often than not, it will extend the time of the awful behavior by generating a whole new sequence of fussing, which is why it's such a loser as a response.

"But why? Why can't I have Leslie over?"
"You know why."
"But you promised. You said Leslie could come over. It's not fair."
"You were warned. You had your chance. But you would not behave."
"But it's not fair. I'll be good. I promise."

Et cetera. Not only that, but there has now been set up a whole probable future fuss when the punishment has to be enforced.

So what can you do?

Not a whole lot. And that can sometimes mean pulling along a tantruming kid through the mall as one goes about one's errands. Usually, but not always, if the tantrum gets no response he or she will at least switch over to a pout.

And if you wish, once you are back in the car or when you reach home, you can express your displeasure.

"Brittany, I am very disappointed. You were awful at the mall. You ruined everybody's time. That was very selfish. I hope you act better next time."

No more than that needs to be said and, unfortunately, it may or may not have an effect on the child's behavior the next time. If a child is consistently awful out in public, parents may want to plan alternatives to taking him or her along. But not taking the child is not always possible, and parents are often stuck in public with a badly behaving child without the same kind of resources they have at home. Unavailable is the number-one option for dealing with awful children: separation.

"Okay, Brittany. You want to fuss. Be my guest. We'll come back and get you here in front of Cookies R Us in half an hour. Bye."

That is definitely not an option. It's too scary for the child and, of course, runs the obvious risks associated with abandoning a child in public.

A fact of child raising:

Some situations are bad, and there is nothing you can do to make them better. But there are lots of things you can do to make them worse. Best is just to get through them.

Critics of Our Parenting

In a supermarket.

Christina, seven, and her mother were waiting in a long line at the checkout counter—people in front, people behind.

"Mommy, would you buy me this?"

Christina had picked up a little yellow plastic egg with cute duckies stenciled on it that was marked 79¢.

"No, Christina, I'm not going to buy you things whenever we are in the supermarket."

"But Mom, it's so cute. Please?"

"I'm sorry. No, Christina. I'm not going to buy you toys when we are in the supermarket."

"Please, Mom? Please?"

"No, Christina."

"But why not, Mommy? Please. It's so cute."

Christina's tone had turned whiny and shrill, and the people in the line were now looking at Christina and her mother and not in a friendly manner.

"Mommy, please. Please. Please. Why not, Mommy? Please. Please. Why not, Mommy?" And Christina started to shriek. "Please! Please! Please!"

"Christina, the answer is 'No'."

Having taken her stand, Christina's mother said no more. From her experience she knew that to give in to Christina at this point would be a mistake and would cost her in supermarket trips to come. Christina's mother definitely wanted to tough it out. But Christina continued to shriek.

Now all the people in line were giving Christina's mother looks that clearly said, "Can't you do something with that child to shut her up? Give her the stupid egg. Smack her. Anything. But SHUT HER UP!"

Christina's mother, with a tantruming child at her feet and hostile supermarket patrons before and behind her, felt very much like someone trying to make a left turn in heavy traffic, unable to find an opening, and cars stacking up behind her beeping their horns.

Then, to top it off, the woman in front of Christina's mother chose to give some helpful advice.

"You know, if she were my child, I wouldn't let her behave that way."

At which point, Christina's mother could not decide among three equally attractive options:

1. Strangling the lady in front of her.
2. Strangling Christina.
3. The most attractive of all—looking for a hole to crawl into and die.

Another story:

Karyn, at her mother's with Ricky, Vicki, and Charlie.

"You know, Karyn, you and Leo never used to act that way. Your father and I would never have let the two of you behave in that manner."
"Mother, you just don't understand. Things are different now. It's not the same as it was when Leo and I were kids."
"Yes, of course. Whatever you say, dear."

It is not easy to bring up children. But what can make it especially tough is that we do not do it in a vacuum. There are all these other people who see what we are doing, have their own thoughts about it, and even say things. Often, these other people are relatives whose opinion we especially care about, even though we wish we did not.

It makes the whole deal harder that we not only have to try to do what is right for us and our children, but we also have to worry about what other people think. We cannot help it. It is part of being human. It can be a problem because it can undermine our confidence in dealing with our own children.

We think:

They do not understand. They are not there every day. They do not know my children—not as I do. They do not know who I am. What works for me. They do not know what I am trying to do. (Even though sometimes they actually are sympathetic and do understand, have kids of their own, and have been in the same kinds of situations many, many times.)

So we try to explain. But we never seem to convince them. Yet there is a solution and that solution is answering for yourself a series of questions:

Who should be making the day-to-day decisions in my child's life?

Who knows more about my child?

Who cares more about my child?

Who is the one who is going to have to live with the consequences of what I do with my child?

Who would I most want to be making the decisions— right or wrong—regarding my child's life?

In truth, we have a choice. We can do what we think is best for our children, what we are most comfortable doing, or we can give in to how it must look to others, what they will say. It is a choice. Which is my top priority—me and my kids, or what others will say or think? If parents in all of the toughest moments can ask themselves this question, it gets easier to come up with the right answer.

Christina's mother in the supermarket waits out the storm —unpleasant as it is. *This is my child, not theirs, and I'm sorry that there are children in the world to make their times in the supermarket sometimes unpleasant. But I happen to have one of those children.*

In front of others whom we love, it turns out that it really is not that hard at all, once you take the first strong stand.

"I'm sorry, Mother, but this is the way I want to do it."

"But Helena, you are really going to spoil him. You'll pay for it. You'll see."

"Mother, I really don't want to talk about it. This is what I am going to do."

"Well, you don't have to be so nasty about it. I was only trying to help."

"I know that, Mother, but I just need to do things my way."

"Well, you didn't have to hurt my feelings."

"I am sorry, Mother."

If one stays with this, surprisingly quickly others do come to respect your authority, though they may still grumble to themselves. After all, it *is* your child, not theirs.

"She really is *spoiling that child."*

And once you start doing it, there comes a nice sense of pride, of being strong, which quiets down these other voices that can make you feel weak.

I may not always be right, but as my children's parent and loving them more than anybody else in the world, I am doing what I in my best judgment—which is the most I can ask of myself—think is right. And who more than I should be, would I want to be, making all those decisions in their lives?

Coming to You with Problems

"Kevin Says He's Going to Beat Me Up"

Six-year-old Conrad one day after school talking to his father:

"Kevin says he's going to beat me up because I said he was a fatso. I didn't say he was a fatso, but he doesn't believe me and now he says he's going to beat me up."

"Well, you know, Conrad, sometimes kids say things to make themselves feel tough. But that doesn't really mean that they're going to do it."

"But he said he was going to beat me up."

"Well, if you're really worried about it, what do you think you could do?"

"I don't know."

"Well, think about it."

"I don't know what to do. I don't want to get beat up."

"Well, maybe you could tell Miss Pritchard and ask her to

talk to the both of you together and maybe it could get settled."

"Do you think that would work?"

"I don't know for sure, Conrad. But that might be a good idea."

"Oh. Okay."

A father helps his son with a problem. But with the day-to-day problems that life throws at a child, how helpful do we want to be? Do we offer solutions as Conrad's father did? Do we work with them to help them find solutions as Conrad's father initially tried to do? Or do we not try to be all that helpful? Do we just listen?

"Kevin says he's going to beat me up because I said he was a fatso. I didn't say he was a fatso, but he doesn't believe me, and now he says he is going to beat me up."

"Oh, sounds like a problem."

"Yeah. I don't want to get beat up."

"I certainly hope you don't get beat up."

"But I don't know what to do."

"Yeah, it really is a problem."

"But you have to help me. Kevin's going to beat me up."

"Gosh, I don't know what to tell you, Conrad. I sure hope things work out."

"But what if they don't work out?"

"Well, that wouldn't be too good."

"But you're supposed to help me."

"Well, things usually have a way of working themselves out, and if it gets to be a big problem, of course I'll help."

"But Kevin says he's going to beat me up tomorrow. That's a big problem. You're no help at all. If he does, it will be your fault."

"Well, I hope he doesn't."

"I'm gonna worry all night."

"I hope not."

"I will."
In reality, what might happen?

(1) Maybe Kevin does beat him up. And, if that became a regular occurrence, maybe Conrad's father would want to intervene. But would he want to intervene in order to avoid one instance of Conrad's getting beat up by a fellow first grader?

(2) It turns out that Kevin—for whatever reason—does not beat him up.

(3) Conrad, on his own, figures out some sort of solution —again, not necessarily the sort of solution we might want.

"Kevin."
"What?"
"It wasn't me who called you a fatso. It was Brian. I heard him. It's true."
"Yeah? I'm gonna beat him up."
"Good. He deserves it."

The question is: What is best in regard to our children's everyday problems?

Give them solutions? Set a model for the *process* of problem solving?

Or, leave it up to them?

The first two options are good, but let me put in a word for some of the benefits of the third option, because it allows for some important lessons. Throwing the problem back to them gives children the burden of having to live with, wrestle with, a problem on their own. They get to experience the discomfort, the struggle, the uncertainty that go with having a problem. Maybe they find a solution, maybe they do not. With that experience, children learn that day-to-day problems, even major problems, have a way of passing by, working themselves out, not being so terrible as one imagined. That they can get from now to then—bridge the gap of what may seem like an insurmountable problem—and come out the other side still in one piece.

"I'm Bored"

> *"Oh. Hi, Jason."*
> *"I'm bored."*
> *"Oh."*
> *"I'm bored. There's nothing to do."*
> *"Did you think about coloring?"*
> *"Coloring is boring."*
> *"Well, sometimes you like it."*
> *"No, I don't. It's boring. There's nothing to do. You do something with me."*
> *"I can't right now, Jason. I'm busy. You'll have to figure out something to do on your own."*
> *"But there is nothing to do."*
> *"What about your Build-O-Straws? You haven't made anything with them for a while. Remember last time, you made that neat fortress. I'll bet you could think of something else like that to build."*
> *"I don't want to. I want you to do something with me."*
> *"I can't, Jason. I'm busy."*
> *"But then there's nothing for me to do. I'm so bored."*

The state of being bored is another of those instances analogous to survival training on a deserted island. Somehow, you have to survive through a segment of time all on your own. Unless children have the practice of getting through time, they become wholly dependent on others to get them through it. Who knows what solution they will come up with? But if left to their own devices, they will come up with something. The time *will* go by.

"Oh. Hi, Jason."
"I'm bored."
"Oh."
"I'm bored. There's nothing to do."

Here Jason's father can make suggestions if he wants. But this early in the sequence, he also can just turn it back to Jason.

"Gee."
"But I'm bored. You have to do something with me."
"No, I'm busy. I guess you'll have to find something your-self."
"But there is nothing. What should I do? I'm bored."
"Gee, that's too bad."
"But you have to do something with me."
"Sorry, Jason. I have to get back to what I'm doing."
"But you can't. You have to do something with me. I'm bored. What should I do? I'm bored. I am."

If Jason's father truly stays out of it, Jason will have to fend for himself and he will find something to do. Perhaps it won't be what his father had in mind.

"Why is the cat howling, Jason?"
"I found a good idea with the Build-O-Straws. I made a cage for Tinkerbell."

Grumpy Children

It really had to do with mornings and breakfast. The gist of it was that in the morning I was usually in a cheerful mood (probably the caffeine kicking in). Nick or Margaret, on the other hand, would often come into breakfast grumpy. But I was in a good mood. Competing moods.

Since I was in a good mood, I refused to participate in their grumpiness. I wanted to continue being cheerful; that was my mood and it was a nice mood to be in.

Consequently, what then took place was a duet. A discordant one. They sang their grumpy melody, I my cheerful one. What I forever afterward thought of as "competing melodies."

A hypothetical example:

James's father had just made breakfast. James's sister Karen was already at the table eating. James entered the kitchen and plunked himself down in front of his nicely made French toast.

"I hate French toast."

"Good morning, my darling," says James's father.

"See, it's soggy."

James's father comes over and gives James a hug and kiss which James sort of shrugs off. "You are my best and biggest guy," says James's father.

James starts eating his French toast.

"Dad, Karen won't pass me the syrup."

James's father says nothing but again comes over and gives another hug and kiss which James again sort of shrugs off. "I sure do love you," says James's father.

"Ouch," says James, accidentally vaguely bumping his elbow on the table.

"*I love French toast. It sure is my favorite. French toast is the king*," sings James's father to no particular tune.

"Dad, you're such a big goof," says James, this time laughing. And the rest of breakfast was very pleasant.

If in fact we go on ignoring their fussing, ignoring their attempt to pull us into their funk, not doing for example:

"I hate French toast."

"But I thought you liked French toast."

"Well, I don't. And this looks gross."

"Well, I am not going to make you something else."

"Well, I am not going to eat this."

Et cetera.

But instead, as did James's father, continue with our happy melody, directly competing with theirs, then, unless they are in a *really* ugly mood, they will usually drop theirs and join in with us. And everybody wins.

It is a particularly pleasant and generally successful way of dealing with the baby self. Its main requirement is that you have to be in a good enough mood to pull it off. But it does work.

It is a method somewhat analogous to responses I described for sulking. A child wants to get into a baby-self snit, but the parents will not join in and instead continue the upbeat flow of their lives, totally heedless of the baby-self attempts to pull them into his or her grumpiness. Here are some examples:

In the car.

"Mommy, Erik keeps pushing me."

"I have an idea. Let's do the license plate game."

"I don't want to. Ooh. Stop that Erik. Mom, he did it again."

Silence. "I have New York and Virginia."

"Mom, he keeps pushing me."

More silence. "New York, Virginia, and New Jersey. That's three."

"That's not fair. You have a head start. Oh, I have New York and Connecticut."

Clement comes into the kitchen.

"But why can't I get a gerbil?" The zillionth time he has asked, having received an explanation half a zillion times.

"Oh, hi, Clement. Would you like to help me?"

"But why? Why can't I get a gerbil?"

"I'm cutting celery. But you can do it if you want. See the size cuts I need. I'm making stuffing for the chicken."

"You're not answering. Why can't I?"

"I haven't cut up the onions yet either. Would you like to do that? I will set you up with a knife and a chopping board."

"Can I use the big knife?"

"Mom, will you set up my paints for me?"

"No. I'm sorry, Evan. I really don't feel like it now."

"But I want to do my paints."

"I will give you a hug if you want."

"I don't want a hug. I want to do paints."

"You can sit on my lap if you want *and* I will give you hugs."

"But I want you to help me with paints."

"My lap is waiting if you want."

"Oh, okay." Evan climbs in his mother's lap and starts sucking his thumb.

"Mom, my stomach still hurts. I don't think I can go to school tomorrow." It always hurts and she always says so on Sunday nights.

"What do you want me to read to you tonight?"

"My stomach hurts."

"I think I'm in the mood for *Stanley and His Pet Prune*. What do you think?"

"My stomach hurts."

"No, maybe the *Magic Galoshes*. We haven't read that in a while."

"No. I want *Stanley and His Pet Prune*."

5

Family Disputes

The art of parenting is in knowing when to engage and when to back off, which includes doing a great deal more of the latter than comes naturally. All of this can become even more complicated when issues are not simply between us and our child—when there are other family members involved as well. As we shall see, the basic rules remain the same. But they are sometimes harder to see in the complex fabric of family life.

Fathers and Mothers—Who's in Charge

Six-year-old Elliot's parents were sitting side by side on the couch. Elliot was cutting up old newspapers with a scissors and starting to make a fairly big mess.

"That's enough, Elliot. I want you to pick up all the news-paper and put away the scissors. You're making too much of a mess," said Elliot's father.

"But I want to play with the newspapers."

"Elliot, I want you to pick up everything now."

"But I don't want to. I'm not making a mess."

"You *are* making a mess. I told you to pick it up."

"But it's not fair. I'm not making a mess. I'm not."

"Elliot, you heard me. You're looking for trouble."

"But it's not fair."

"Oh, for goodness sakes, Rusty. Let him play with the newspapers. He's not hurting anything. And now he's all upset," said Elliot's mother, growing aggravated by the unfolding scene.

"You stay out of this, Angie. You're always contradicting me in front of Elliot. He knows that if he makes a fuss, you'll always come running to take his side."

"That's not true, Rusty. It's just that you make such unreasonable demands on him. And then the two of you get into these battles. It's awful to have to listen to you."

"Yeah, well, you won't have to listen to me. You win, Elliot. Mommy saved you again." And Elliot's father stormed out of the room.

The basic rule of two-person parenting is:

If one parent is involved in limit setting, the other should stay out of it.

The second parent should not intervene, except where there is threat of harm, even if he or she feels that what the first parent is doing is definitely wrong. Get involved only if you're invited.

"Would you handle this, Angie?" If Angie accepts, *she* would now be in charge.

But a parent never wants to intervene at the invitation of the child:

"Mommy, I can keep playing, right? I'm not hurting anything, right?"

"Well, he's asking me, Rusty, and I think it's okay."

Angie's intervention at the request of Elliot would only undermine his father's authority. Angie's only response to Elliot's request must be:

"No. Your father says 'No.' And that's it."

Or perhaps, "That's between you and your father."

Parents *must* back up each other.

And if not invited to take over, Angie must let the scene be played out without her participation, *regardless* of the conclusion.

"You yell at me. That's all you ever do."

"I've had it with you, Elliot."

As messily as this scene ended, if Angie had interfered and contradicted her husband, her actions clearly would have said to Elliot, "Your father is not the final authority. I am."

That immediately creates a number of real problems, such as:

1. Dissension between parents.

    "Why can't you stay out of it when I'm dealing with Elliot? He's my kid, too, you know."

    "I would if you weren't always so unreasonable with him."
2. Inevitable resentment of the interfered-with parent toward the child.

    "He always runs to her. And of course she is on his side."
3. Bypassing of one parent.

"I don't have to deal with Daddy. If I don't like what's going on between me and him, I can go to Mommy."

When Angie routinely undermines the authority of Rusty, the relationship between Rusty and his son is automatically damaged. If there is no interference, Rusty and Elliot are free to work out the destiny of their relationship on their own. From Rusty's standpoint, he will have no grudge against Elliot other than what happens between them. The relationship at least has a chance to evolve, for better or worse. But this can happen only where Elliot and his father can test their relationship unimpeded.

Perhaps the major benefit will be to Elliot. He will have to learn to fend for himself in his relationship with his father, a difficult arena for many fathers and sons. And so long as his father is not truly abusive, he will survive. Elliot might come to like his father, and their relationship could be a major one in his life. But he might also grow to dislike his father, and to dislike a father who is not nice is not necessarily bad.

Regardless of the ultimate fate of the relationship, Elliot will feel that, in this special realm of father and son, he managed all on his own and can respect himself.

"I can deal with Dad. I can be with him, take whatever he throws at me, and come out the other end still me. I do not fear him. Sometimes he makes me feel bad, but I can handle it. I am strong."

If there is physical abuse, the other parent *must* intervene to protect the child. If such interference dooms the relationship between child and abusing parent, so be it. But where the abuse is only harsh words, the need for intervention from the other parent for the sake of the child is not as clear. Verbal abuse can be damaging, but it's hard to know what children can handle and what they cannot. It's therefore hard to know whether to intervene or not. Plus, there are risks with either decision: damage to the children versus damage to their relationship with the verbally abusive parent

But if a parent chooses not to intervene directly, he or she still can be of use.

"You little jerk. Don't you have any sense?" says her mother to Isabel.

"Daddy, am I a jerk? Mom always calls me a jerk."

"No, you're not a jerk. Mom says that because she's mad. But you're not a jerk."

Just these few words can go a long way to restoring self-respect. The child is given significant support in dealing with a verbally abusive parent without direct interference from the other parent.

"I'm not a jerk. She only *says* I'm a jerk. *She's* a jerk for saying I'm a jerk."

It can take out much of the sting.

Playing One Parent against the Other

"But Daddy said I didn't have to go outside," says Quinlan to his mother. Quinlan's statement is a lie, but at that moment his father is running an errand and unavailable for verification.

When children deviously manipulate their parents to get matters to go their way, they are behaving like normal children. That is what children do, but parents need not worry because there is a fairly simple and effective response to such deviousness.

1. If the other parent is not there to check with, then your child is stuck with you.

"I'm sorry, Quinlan. Your dad's not here. I want you outside."

"But it's not fair. Dad said I didn't have to. Wait until he gets home. It's not fair."

"I'm sorry. I'm here and I want you outside."

"No, it's not fair."

"Outside. Now, Quinlan."

2. If the other parent is there, check.

"Did you say Quinlan didn't have to go outside?"

"Yeah, it's sorta muddy."

At that point, the second parent has the option of backing off.

"Okay, Quinlan. I guess you don't have to go out."
"Great. You're a great mom."

Or disagreeing.

"No, I think he should go out. Otherwise he'll just be in all day and watch TV."

The parents can then negotiate *briefly*. Their resolution does not matter as long as they invoke the parental decision-making rules and decide quickly one way or the other:

"No, I think your mother is right. You should go outside."
"No, Dad. No. Don't give in to her. Stand up for yourself. You're right. It is muddy."
"Outside, Quinlan."
"I hate both of you. Cough. Cough. I think I have a cold. I can tell it's going to get worse."

3. If a child gets away with the deception and is found out, confront him with his deviousness.

"Your father did not say you could stay in. You lied, Quinlan. And I don't like that."
"I didn't lie. He said so. He doesn't remember."
"I don't like you being sneaky like that."

The main point of the confrontation for Quinlan is that his parents are in communication. He sees that there is a limit to the success of his deviousness. Should they make a big deal about his sneakiness, the dishonesty, the lying? No. But this is a major subject that I'll discuss in full shortly. In regard to the sort of deviousness described here, the parents' job is to be on top of it as best they can. And if once in a while the sneakiness is successful and Quinlan's deviousness is rewarded, so what.

Parental Arguments

What about parental arguments? Cannot their arguing, in and of itself, be bad for children? Perhaps, but probably not. Parental arguments are an inevitable part of one's childhood and these arguments, even where there is much noise, are not bad as long as:

1. The arguments do not turn violent.
2. They do not lead to a separation—one parent moving out.
3. They are not constant.
4. They are not overly demeaning—one parent to the other.
5. They do not involve the children as participants or as peacemakers.

"Mommy, Mommy, please stop fighting, please. Don't get a divorce. Please stop fighting," sobs little Jenny. And her parents, seeing how upsetting the fighting is to her, stop their arguing.

The above scene is not okay. When parents fight, children must feel powerless. They cannot influence what is going on or stop it. They need to feel that it is transpiring at a level beyond them, above them, in the big adult world to which they have no entry. Though highly tempting food to the baby self (the food that does not nurture), entering the adult world is also ultimately terrifying. When children are allowed to cross over into the adult world, they are faced with responsibilities far beyond what they can handle. But when they know that what they say or do cannot deeply affect or change Mommy or Daddy, they are allowed to feel like the children they are.

"Get out of here, Jenny. This is between Mommy and me."
"But I'm so scared. I hate it when you fight. I'm so scared."
"Good-bye, Jenny."

Jenny must go off for the duration of her parents' fight and wait it out alone. She'll survive. She is safe and her parents are there should anything serious happen.

If parents can argue within the limits I suggested above, their arguments will be seen by their children as perhaps noisy and unpleasant, but not especially relevant to them. If parents can argue within limits, children learn that adults *can* argue and nothing terrible happens. People can fight and, when it is over, things can go back to normal. To their children, parents' fighting can truly become no big deal.

I wish they would stop the arguing so I can get back into the TV room.

"Excuse me. Excuse me."

"What is it, Jenny?"

"Could you two please argue in the kitchen?"

Sibling Fighting

Nine-year-old Donald and seven-year-old Daniel were watching TV in the family room when a fight broke out over who was hogging space on the couch. Shortly, Daniel ran out of the room crying with his older brother in pursuit. Daniel ran directly to his father.

"Donald won't let me sit on the couch and he keeps hitting me and he twisted my arm real hard and I think he broke it."

"Danny's such a liar. He kept kicking me. I wasn't doing anything."

"I did not. Donald's the one that's lying."

"I'm going to slam you, Danny."

"See, Dad, see."

At this point, the perfect father says:

"Calm down, boys. Donald. Danny. Now I want each of

you to tell me what went on. One at a time, and no inter-
rupting. Now Donald, you first."

The father then listens quietly to both sides, hearing each
child fully. Then, after thinking about what they have said,
he suggests a solution that would be fair to both—though each
would have to concede a little. By this procedure, the father
helps the children learn to listen and to deal with everyday
situations in a fair and reasonable manner. He provides not
only a solution to the immediate issue, but also a model for
future problem solving.

Both boys then return to watching television, feeling that
their needs have been met, that they have been listened to,
and that their father's solution, though not totally to their
liking, can be lived with.

This little story, of course, could take place only among the
Phalni (three-foot-high wasplike creatures) on the planet Tril-
gon III of the Protus Alpha Star System. Nowhere else within
the known universe could it actually happen.

My Sisters and I

I remember a car trip my family took along the Shenandoah
Drive in Virginia. We were in a car for 300 miles in heavy
fog that blotted out any scenery. I also remember there were
no rest stops for those 300 miles! (Is this possible?) By agree-
ment of all who were there, it was the ultimate actualization
of hell on earth. Yet it was not much worse than what went
on every day among my two sisters, Mary and Ellen, and me.
Bickering, arguing, screaming, case pleading, and outraged
tantrums were necessary and normal. Ellen and I didn't battle
that much, but that was only because we were too busy engaging with Mary, the baby of the family who had the triple
advantage that she was younger, physically smaller and thin-

ner, and also could cry easily. Like many adult siblings, the three of us are now quite friendly and our relationships are basically devoid of squabbling.

I mention the fighting among the three of us as children because it is what gave me the strong resolve to try to figure out and stay with some plan with my children that might head off the truly ghastly and incessant bickering I had taken part in, despite the best efforts of our intelligent and genuinely caring parents. I wanted my wife, Mary Alice, and I to do the opposite of whatever my parents did.

What We Did

What we came up with—and we followed this plan right from the start—was as follows: Unless it seemed that either Nick or Margaret was in real danger of getting hurt, we would never intervene on one side or the other. If they came to us because of an argument, we would *never* listen. We were especially strict about truly not listening.

"*I do not want to hear about it.*"

If we did have to intervene, both children were in trouble, regardless of the circumstances. Interventions were made only where one child might injure the other. "No, you cannot poke her in the eye." It is a good message. The *only* crime that is bad enough, serious enough, to single out one for blame is injury to another.

But those interventions were to prevent injury, not pain.

"Nicky hit me."

"I don't want to hear about it."

And if there was risk of injury, then who started the fight was definitely not at issue.

"*You cannot poke Margaret in the eye.*"

"*But she kicked me and she messed up my baseball cards.*"

"*You cannot poke Margaret in the eye.*"

Interventions were also made when their fighting was too irritating to us. But then they both had to suffer the consequences, which usually meant getting yelled at, and if that failed to stop the fighting, then both were banished to separate places. Again, we paid no attention to who was at fault, and when they would try to plead their cases to us, we absolutely would not listen.

I even had a rule (I am not sure if Mary Alice used a similar rule) that if one told on the other—"Nicky poured his milk down the sink"—I would do nothing, even if the transgression was something for which Nicky normally would have gotten yelled at. I considered the information, in view of its source, inadmissible evidence.

Later, I even had a rule that if one told on the other, the one *told on* got a nickel. I will not defend or recommend this rule—I invoked it only once or twice—except to say that I liked it and so did Nick and Margaret.

Over time, Nick and Margaret basically gave up trying to tell us who started it, whose fault it was, because they *never* got listened to. In truth, Nick and Margaret may have fought as much as other children. But what was absent was the constant bickering, the constant involving of us in their squabbles—whose fault it was, how we were not fair, how we always took one or the other's side. Over the course of Nick's and Margaret's childhoods, Mary Alice and I did not have to endure that kind of bickering, and it made a huge difference. Being with the two of them together was almost always fun.

The Truth about Sibling Fighting

The truth about sibling fighting is that one can either train one's children to work it out themselves or one can train them to rely on a parent to work things out for them. Should parents become the resolvers of arguments, they will find that arguments rarely get resolved. Instead, parents will invariably find themselves caught up in the ongoing squabbling, with clean and satisfying solutions the unusual exception. All their children will learn is expertise in case pleading.

There *is* a solution to the problem of sibling fighting. It is not a solution that eliminates the fighting, though it does reduce its frequency and intensity. But it enormously reduces the wear and tear on parents, and significantly changes for the better the actual feelings between brothers and sisters.

The Rules for Sibling Fighting

The rules are as follows:

Unless there is a real risk of somebody getting hurt, a parent should not intervene on one side or the other in their children's fights—ever.

And since a parent is not going to take one side or the other, then a parent should not act as a judge in disagreements—ever.

Most important, since a parent is not going to act as a judge, then, when children come running with conflicting stories in the heat of an argument, a parent should not listen—ever.

"James smashed my Lego fort, and I spent two hours making it."

"I did not. Carly was pinching me, right on where I have a sore elbow."

"I do not want to hear about it."

"But now my elbow hurts real bad."

"I didn't touch his elbow."

"I do not want to hear about it."

It's Their Choice

A result of the above practice is that children are made to work things out on their own. If they cannot, then parents may have to intervene. But then all involved will be the losers.

"You can't watch TV without squabbling? Then nobody watches TV."

They have a choice. Somehow work things out, or risk parental wrath and consequences. This strategy puts the burden on the children. Somehow they must not let matters get too out of hand or everyone will suffer. It eliminates: "If we can't work things out, we'll go to Mommy or Daddy." With parents removed, children often do work things out. Even if they don't succeed completely, they learn limits beyond which they must not push each other. Many times they get out of hand anyway, and parents have to intervene. But this will happen less often if the rules for intervention are followed.

One test of our policy was Saturday morning cartoons. At the time, we had only one television and Nick and Margaret, as invariably will happen, did not always want to watch the same program. But rather than our getting involved and working out some fair schedule for sharing (which I have no objection to parents doing), we chose to have them work it out on their own. The only rule was that if there was so much squabbling that we were disturbed, then there would be no TV at all. I do not know what they worked out. All I know is that, with exceptions so rare that I cannot remember them, they did work out something because each Saturday they both watched, together. If there was squabbling, I was unaware of it.

Sibling Rivalry

Perhaps the most important result of the above practice is its effect on the feelings between brothers and sisters. If sibling squabbling pulls the parents into the roles of judge and jury, then the whole nature of the relationship between the siblings changes. The nature of the change is very simple. Let us say that there is an argument between a brother and a sister over who gets the choice of television show. If parents do not get involved in the argument, and the argument stays within bounds of noise or violence, then the worst that can happen is that one child may not get to watch the show he or she wants. However, if parents get involved as arbiters, everything changes. Now added into the argument over which television show to watch is the question of whose side their parents will be on.

The problem is that whose side one's parents take is a very powerful issue for all children. Plainly and simply, it is a direct food call to the baby self. It is so powerful, in fact, that the original issue of getting to watch a desired television show pales in comparison. Conflicts between siblings then leave the original arena and become battles for parental favor. The wants of the baby self are so much more powerful, they rout the brother-and-sister argument. All that remain are two voracious baby selves looking for their next feeding. Dueling baby selves.

"I didn't ever, Mom. He's lying."
"She did, Mom. She took it. She's the one who's lying."

There is no way around it: Parental side-taking injects into all day-to-day dealings between brothers and sisters the very powerful issue of parental favor. They are not pitted against each other about who gets to watch a particular TV show— small potatoes. They are now battling for their parents' support. Very big stuff indeed. The bottom line is that most of the genuine ill will that exists between siblings is a direct product of being constantly pitted against one another in the battle for parental favor.

A common phenomenon—it happened with my two sisters and me—is that children who fight bitterly throughout childhood and even genuinely hate each other during those years (or at least that is the only feeling they are in touch with) find to their surprise that when they leave their parental home, now with no parents to compete over, suddenly they get along fine. Yet all during their childhoods the rivalry may have been intense.

Sibling Fighting and the Baby Self

One of the major and especially successful tools of the baby self in its perpetual quest to get as much and as passionate parental involvement as possible is the provoking of sibling fighting. To this end, the baby self is ever cunning, and fast on its feet.

Delbert, bored, had started whining at his mother about his ongoing need for a Mega Man III, but his real hope was that he might engage her in an extended fuss.

"But I need a Mega Man III. You have to buy me one."
"No, Delbert. And do not keep pestering me about it."

And Delbert's baby self, feeling that this particular parent provocation tack was not working, immediately went over and started bothering his brother, who was playing quietly by himself. "Mom, Delbert ripped my paper."

"I did not. D.J. won't let me use his Magic Marker."

"Delbert, leave D.J. alone."

Delbert's baby self senses a possible winner.

"But he won't share the Magic Markers. Mom, it's not fair."

"You're just going to have to leave him alone."

"But, Mom . . . he never shares anything."

"I do too share," pipes in D.J., now entering the fray to the cheering of Delbert's baby self.

"No, Mom, D.J.'s lying, he never shares."

"You two are going to have to learn to share."

In the realm of sibling fighting and fairness (already discussed as one of the most treasured items in the baby self's arsenal), the baby self moves into the sublime.

James and Jeanine's father had equally dealt out a bag of M&M's. Each child got thirty-six and their father ate the odd-numbered one.

"It's not fair. James got more yellows."

At that moment, if we were to interview Jeanine, "Do you really care so much that James got two more yellows than you did?" she would say "Yes. It's not fair," her face flushing with impassioned indignation. And our lie detector would show her telling the truth. Yet before that moment of dividing the M&M's, Jeanine did not even know that she preferred yellow ones.

Indeed, parents who genuinely try to be fair more often than not find themselves sucked deeper and deeper into a morass of sibling litigation where ultimately nothing is resolved and everybody is angry. Except the baby selves who conjointly are enjoying the excellent food at the picnic.

If children are left on their own, they work things out most of the time. But the basis for their resolutions is more often "what I can live with" than fairness. These resolutions are not always what we would have chosen, but they are necessary compromises and useful rules for living nonetheless.

"I actually don't mind Kevin punching me, so long as I get to call him a 'retard'."

"I don't mind Sarah taking my clothes without asking and sometimes ruining them, so long as I can hit her and make her cry when she ruins something I really like."

"Yes, Sherri beats me up sometimes. But I get to wear her clothes."

The strict rules of fairness do have their place in the world, but for the most part they are learned elsewhere.

Big Bullies, Little Victims?

If brothers and sisters are left to work things out on their own, won't the bigger and older invariably bully the younger and littler, and won't that have a bad effect on the smaller child?

This is almost certainly the main and valid concern with the system of dealing with sibling fighting advocated here.

Nine-year-old Isaiah is a lot bigger and stronger than his seven-year-old brother, Joshua. What is to stop Isaiah from constantly bullying Joshua if his parents never intervene except when Isaiah might risk injury to his younger brother, or when the two of them are making too much noise?

"That's it, you two."
"But Isaiah is beating me up."
"I said stop it or you go to your rooms."

If that is the deal, why won't Isaiah simply hit Joshua whenever the mood strikes him, totally tyrannize his brother, use whatever he wants of Joshua's without asking permission, and make Joshua do his bidding by physically intimidating him? The answer is simple: If parental favor is *truly* taken out of the arena in fights between siblings, they have no deep reason to dislike one another. They will fight, irritate each other, get in each other's way, but there will also be a place for affection and for the mature part of them—for their true sense of fairness and consideration—to enter into the relationship.

At times, Isaiah will bully Joshua, will take out his own personal frustrations by beating on his brother. At times, Isaiah will use his superior size and strength to intimidate his younger brother. But if Joshua never runs to his parents crying "Isaiah hit me" and the parent admonishes Isaiah, "How many times do we have to tell you? Stop picking on Joshua!"; if, when Joshua does complain, the complaint falls on deaf ears; if, when Isaiah and Joshua end up in a fight that does get out of hand, with Isaiah definitely overpowering but *not injuring* his brother, they get yelled at equally with no parental interest in fault or blame; if all of the above are true, then the greatest impediment to the older sibling's liking the younger one and acting, some of the time, in a mature fashion will be removed. If Isaiah understands that his younger brother, simply by being the smaller and weaker, cannot automatically get his parents on his side, the way is then cleared for Isaiah to like Joshua, and at times to act toward him in a mature manner.

Isaiah will feel that he can use his bigger size as an advantage over his younger brother if he wants to, and he will feel good about it. But Isaiah *is* older, bigger, and more powerful than Joshua. Why should he not be allowed to feel good about it? Because Isaiah is allowed to feel more powerful than Joshua, he is also free to act charitably toward his brother, occasionally, when he feels like it.

Isaiah will bully Joshua. But he will also like Joshua. There are no overriding baby-self issues at stake. And the bullying will be contained—not stopped—by his affection for his little brother and by the intervention of his mature self, which can at times come to the fore. In real life it really does work this way.

But what about Joshua? Is he not the victim? Will he not suffer from it? Will he not be damaged?

Not really. Joshua will not be completely defenseless. He will get his licks in. If he is like most younger siblings, he will figure out ways to tease and aggravate Isaiah. Even though it may be at the risk of getting punched, he will at times do it anyway—quite possibly choosing those times when a parent is handy at least to run and hide behind.

Still, Joshua will be genuinely bullied at times with no recourse for revenge. Occasionally, he will be more or less at the mercy of his older brother. It is not fun to be bullied. There are moments when Joshua will desperately resent his older brother and will rue the fact that he is smaller and weaker. But Isaiah's power to bully Joshua is limited. His parents will intervene to protect Joshua from serious harm. The true power, where the bigger, more significant lessons of restraint and consideration are taught, is of course with their parents.

Though Joshua will feel less powerful in regard to his big brother, he will not feel one bit less loved or favored by his parents. Feeling loved by one's parents, far more than anything else, gives Joshua his sense of self-worth. Joshua may at times hate being smaller than Isaiah, especially when he gets picked on, but he will also feel that in their parents' eyes he and Isaiah are on equal footing. They are both valued and loved.

But the main reason that sometimes being bullied is ultimately not a serious problem for Joshua lies in a fact of human nature, a phenomenon regularly observed by parents. Little ones tend to idolize, to love their big brothers and sisters. Little ones do genuinely hate it when they get picked on and they do genuinely suffer, but this doesn't seem to stop them from loving their big brother or sister anyway. They do not seem deterred from immediately approaching their bigger sibling once an unpleasant incident has ended. This is especially true if there are times when the bigger sibling is nice and enjoys his younger brother or sister. This will almost always happen when the older sibling does not have a deep grievance against his younger brother, such as "Joshua can always get Mom on his side because he's little."

Most parents have certainly witnessed the speed with which a younger sibling, recently pummeled or ridiculed into heartbroken despondency, can swiftly recover and seek to reengage.

"Isaiah, will you play a game with me?"

Which, in fact, Isaiah may be disposed to do. Having only minutes before reduced his brother to tears, but having no outstanding grievance against him, Isaiah may at that point play with his brother.

Are the little ones traumatized or just upset? Are they damaged by the bullying or do they just strongly dislike it? Can they cope? Can they truly rebound and not be damaged? To witness them in action, it certainly looks as if they can.

But might they not internalize the abuse? Might it not actually damage their self-image?

Ingrid, nine, often temperamental, was frequently disposed to taking out her bad moods on her five-year-old sister, Sonya.

"That drawing's awful. You're going to have to learn to draw. You're so stupid."

And at such times, Sonya—described by her mother as the "gentlest little dumpling"—would just take it, sitting there saying nothing. But then her lower lip would start to quiver. And then she would burst into sobs.

"It is so sad when Ingrid puts her down like that," Sonya's mother would say, "because Sonya really looks up to Ingrid. Sonya so much takes it to heart."

Does Sonya take it to heart? Does it become part of her self-image? *"I'm a bad drawer. I'm dumb."*

Or are put-downs by another sibling something a little different? Is there a realm of sibling abuse that children ultimately learn not to take so seriously? Though initially hurt by their sisters' words, the Sonyas of the world do learn that what sisters say, even idolized big sisters, can often be nothing more than groundless attempts to get them upset. Not statements of true character flaws by a knowing judge, but aggravating jabs, similar to a pinch or a hair pull with no more meaning than that. Gradually, in time, the Sonyas learn to speak up for themselves.

"I am not a bad drawer. You're a bad drawer."

There is a process that children learn if we let them, whereby they develop a certain toughness, a certain counterpunching ability, that allows them to deal with critical jabs and not always to be victims, not to be hurt by the *normal* unpleasantnesses of day-to-day life. This toughness—not taking everything to heart, not taking everything personally—is necessary for dealing well with the everyday world. We want to produce children who can stand up for themselves, who in the face of adversity do not crumble in despair. Sonya's mother would want to do all she could to develop this ability. She would want Sonya to get such training. And what better training for such skills than fending off a verbally abusive older sister?

"Sonya, your breath smells."
"Yours smells worse."

Even if the day-to-day abuse between siblings is not physically harmful, when it becomes truly damaging to one or the other, then we must intervene. But if it does not, maybe in time they can learn to handle it because it is all in the realm of two baby selves dishing it out, and both baby selves know that none of it counts, none of it is serious.

"You're *a butt brain*."
"You're *a butt brain*."

If Parents Aren't There:
A Witnessed Scene and a Question

As I worked on this section, outside my motel room three children began playing shuffleboard—two girls about twelve years old and a nine-year-old boy, apparently the brother of one of the girls. There were no parents anywhere in evidence.

"Teach me how to play," said the boy.

"No, watch. You'll learn," said his sister.

"Teach me," said the boy.

"Just watch."

Not satisfied, the boy went over and grabbed up one of the shuffleboard pucks.

"Fine. We'll play without it. You're such a baby."

The boy took the puck and sat on a low wall nearby. The girls started to play.

The boy flung the puck in a direction away from the girls.

"You *have* to teach me," he said.

"Just watch and you'll learn," said his sister.

The boy retrieved the puck and threw it toward his sister.

"Catch."

He then sat down next to the shuffleboard court and watched the girls play.

I noticed them again maybe ten minutes later. The girls apparently had been playing and the boy watching them play.

"You said three innings and then it was my turn to play. You've played four."

"No we haven't."

"Yes you have. This is the fourth."

"One was warm-up. *This* is the third," said his sister.

The boy, not buying it, leaped up from his chair, took four

of the pucks and ran away with them shouting, "I'm not giving them back."

The boy then threatened to drop them in the swimming pool.

"You'll get in trouble."

The boy didn't drop the pucks in the pool, but glared at his sister. The girls walked away. The boy, holding his pucks, watched.

The girls stopped and turned.

"Are you going to give us the pucks?"

"One more inning and that's it," said the boy, flinging the pucks back to them.

The question: What would have happened if there had been parents around?

I leave the answer up to my reader's imagination.

Divorce

For better or worse, we live in a world where marriages often end in divorce. Divorce is a fact of life for today's kids. What should parents do if they are getting, or are already, divorced? What effect does divorce have on children? This is a big and complex topic. The following discussion cannot deal with all the issues involved. I have focused on what I think are some of the major concerns that regularly come up for children when parents divorce.

Telling Them

If you are thinking about getting a divorce, but only thinking about it, discussing that possibility with your children is not useful. All it does is set up an ongoing worry that will intrude on their day-to-day lives, and about which they can do nothing.

Only when parents know that divorce or separation is definitely going to happen should they tell their children.

The idea of their parents getting a divorce is very scary to children. It is like the bottom dropping out of their lives; all that was stable goes into free fall. Divorce is the dissolution of their world as they know it. Therefore, when children are told that something so disrupting is going to become a reality, they need to know what this unknown terror is actually going to look like. What children above all care about knowing and what they need to know is:

What is going to happen? What is going to happen to me? Where will I live? Where will Mommy and Daddy live? Will I get to see them? Where will my brothers and sisters live? When will it happen?

Tell them the basics as accurately as possible. Tell them what is going to happen and when it will happen. Tell them what the new living arrangements will be. Tell them what the probable arrangements for seeing each parent will be. And if you are unsure what will happen, tell them this:

"We are getting a divorce, but we are not certain what the exact living arrangements will be. We still have to work that out. But we will tell you as soon as we know anything for sure."

Initially, make the discussions you have with them brief, because what they are hearing can be overwhelming. You want to provide the basics and then allow them to react and to digest, as well as they can for now, the very unsettling news that they are hearing.

Parents do *not* want to get into lengthy discussions about why the separation or divorce is occurring. For most situations, short and simple discussions of the reasons suffice.

"Your father and I have not been getting along for a long time. And now we both feel this is best."

"You know how your mother and I are always arguing. We both feel that we no longer can live together."

Parents never want to involve their children in discussions about the whys and wherefores, the slights, wrongs, faults, problems, inadequacies, and dishonesties of the other parent, except for statements of facts that are obvious.

"Did Dad leave you for Vivian?" It's obvious that indeed their father has left for Vivian.

"Yes. He did."

But not lots of details. Discussions and answers should always be honest, simple, straightforward, and, whenever possible, not about areas of adult concern.

But some children will do all they can to get involved, to learn everything they can about the inner workings of their parents' breakup.

"Is Daddy leaving because you weren't nice enough to him?"

"What went on was between me and your father."

It is never in their best interest to let children in at that level. Divorce resides in the world of adult concerns and is beyond what they can handle. Despite their sometimes intense interest in that world, their involvement can only serve to interfere with the normal healthy functioning of their lives.

But in regard to the breakup, there actually are some issues that children need to know. If they do not ask, it doesn't hurt to question them.

"Arthur, do you sometimes think that maybe you had something to do with me and your mother breaking up?"

Children often worry about this, frequently taking responsibility for what occurred, when that is far from the truth. But you can see how it could happen.

"Yes, we did do a lot of arguing about you. But no, that is not why we separated. We separated because we couldn't get along. Dad and I would still have our problems even if you were perfect, which you are not supposed to be."

Raising the topic gives them the opportunity to voice their worries, which can be a great relief. They no longer have to harbor a guilty secret:

I was the cause of my parents' divorce.

Over the following days, weeks, and months, be readily available to listen should they have questions. Occasionally ask them. Don't wait for them to come to you, because some will and some won't.

"Jeremy, is there anything you want to talk to me about or ask me about Dad and me getting a divorce?"

Ask this regularly even if they do not seem interested.

"No, nothing."

But keep asking so they know that it is an open invitation.

As I have said, ideally one does not want to have children worrying for an extended period of time about the *possibility* of their parents getting a divorce, but sometimes it is unavoidable. For example, in a family where a divorce is a real possibility and the children overhear a big argument with threats or discussion of divorce, it is not useful to sidestep what may be too obvious and ultimately real.

"No, don't worry about it, dear" will far more likely create deeper anxiety. The parent's denial simply will not be believed. Rather, in those circumstances it is best to say:

"I don't know. I hope not. But if we do, you do not have to worry. You will always have one of us to live with."

When parents divorce, it can be helpful to consult a professional counselor. Counseling can help parents deal better with their children in regard to divorce issues, and it can provide a neutral person to whom children can express their fears and concerns and who can perhaps help them adjust to a difficult time in their lives.

Children Taking Sides

One set of parents:

"Mom said that you left the marriage because you were having an affair with Cecily, and that if it wasn't for that, you and she would still be married."

Their mother drives me crazy. She is such a liar. She doesn't mention her affair with Fred Dirkner three years ago. She doesn't mention that she hasn't had sex with me in the last two years of our marriage. (I mean, I know I shouldn't say that.) But she doesn't mention how she just got madder and madder at me all the time—about anything—which was the real problem, the reason why we broke up.

Yes, I had the affair with Cecily. But that was not until after Jill and I had decided to separate. Cecily and I had started to care about each other before that, but, yes, even then it was long dead between me and Jill.

Another set of parents:

"Dad says you were too interested in having a good time and not enough in being a mother, which is why you and he got the divorce. He also says you shouldn't go out so much Saturday nights and leave us with sitters."

That creep! He never cared about the kids—or me. All he ever cared about was having a neat house and quiet kids to come home to.

Children don't want to take sides. What they want and what absolutely is in their best interest is to be left free to preserve the idea that both parents love them, are good, and are deserving of their love. If one or the other parent treats them badly—excluding abuse—they will make their own judgments about their relationship with that parent: Me and Dad. Me and Mom.

I do not want to have to report to Mom what goes on at Dad's. I do not want to feel that I have to watch what I say at Mom's because Dad would be mad if he knew that I said it.

I want it to be separate. I don't want to hear about what one thinks about the other. I don't want to have to take sides.

Sometimes it can be very hard to resist pulling our children into the battle—especially where the other parent does not seem to be playing by these rules at all. One does so much want to set the record straight. But as I said, parents want to avoid involving their children. If you feel you absolutely have to respond, then use short one-sentence disclaimers at the most:

"No, the marriage did not end because of me and Cecily."

But it's best just not to get into it at all.

"I'm sorry your mother feels that way."

"But did it end because of you and Cecily?"

"It's just not something I'm going to talk about."

Parents find it strange that kids accept this, but they do. They don't care if their father had an affair with Cecily before the marriage ended. All they care about is that the marriage ended and whether the parents will get back together. Fault is not an issue they seek out. If their father makes it clear that at least with him they are "off the case," they will happily and gratefully accept their dismissal and get back to childhood concerns.

Nor do children like to be messengers, conduits of information back and forth between parents, because then they are pulled back into the relationship that exists between their parents, which is not where they want or need to be.

"Mom says that the child-support check will be late this month, but you should get it by the fifteenth."

There is a definite consolation for those who can keep their children out of it. With most divorces, there comes a day of reckoning, usually when the children get to be teenagers or young adults. They come to view all that is going on and all that went on with changed, adult eyes. And from that perspective what went on can look very different.

"I now see that you were the strong one. You were the one that was able to keep me out of all that stuff between you and Mom, which I hated to get involved in. But Mom was always involving me. I feel mad at her for doing that. Maybe I feel bad for her. But you I respect for having kept me out of it."

At the Other Parent's

Their father never grew up. He is totally irresponsible. When he has the kids I don't know what goes on. I don't know what kind of supervision they have. And I've heard the kids describe some of the people he has over. I worry about them the whole time they are at their father's.

A different parent:

Since the divorce, their mother has become extremely religious. When the kids are over there she wants them to follow all of the religious rules that she does. And she preaches at them—a lot of stuff that I don't believe in at all, that I don't want them to feel they have to believe.

One very real problem with divorce is that the other parent of your children can be someone whom you do not think well of anymore. But that person is still a full legal parent of *your* child, and there are times (most of the time, in fact, if he or she has main physical custody) when your children are with the other parent and fully under the other parent's control and influence. And you feel that what the other parent may do could be damaging to your child.

"Mom, Dad says I was stupid because I got a bad grade in reading."

The temptation is to put one's hand in and somehow change it.

"Harry, did you say that James was stupid because of his bad grade? You know how the school says he has low self-esteem."

"Gosh, Phyllis, I'm glad you pointed that out to me. I'll try to be more considerate of James's feelings. Thanks."

In real life, of course, it just doesn't work that way. Even comments like "Your Dad shouldn't say that" are tricky. Bad-mouthing the other parent becomes part of taking sides. Far better:

"Do you think you're stupid?"

"I don't know."

"Well, I don't think you're stupid. I know you try. And that's what's important."

Whether you like it or not, the other parent will also have an influence on your child; there is no way around it. The best course for both parents is to be the best parent possible during the time they are with their child.

But their father can be cruel sometimes.

Unless there is reason to suspect actual abuse or genuine neglect, in which case one must intervene through legal channels, there really is little that you can or want to do.

But Juan always says he doesn't like going over to his father's and stepmother's on the weekends. That they hardly ever pay any attention to him. That he is bored a lot. And they are very strict.

Often it is hard to know, even from what children say, what is really going on. Is Juan trying to say what he thinks his mother wants to hear? Is he looking for sympathy and extra goodies from his mother? But let us say that Juan consistently does have an unenjoyable time whenever he goes over to his father's. Do such times at the other parent's house *hurt* a child?

The rule here is similar to what one does as the in-house parent, which is back off—unless there is abuse—and let them work out their own destinies. If the time is generally unpleasant for them, there is an independence and a strength gained just from having gotten through it. Like the logo on a T-shirt: I survived another boring weekend at Dad's and mean Sylvia's.

Different Rules, Different Houses

But I don't agree with what he does with them. They have completely different rules over there, and then Gregory and Jeannette expect me to treat them the same way here. Gregory drives me crazy. "Dad says we can stay up until nine-thirty. Why can't we here? You're mean."

All of which is simply not a problem. As discussed earlier, rules for children need not be the same from place to place, from person to person, a fact of life children readily learn and accept. But that does not mean that they won't test the rules anyway.

"But Dad says we *are* old enough to stay up till nine-thirty."

"Gosh, Gregory, how nice for you that you get to stay up at your father's until nine-thirty. But here your bedtime is eight-thirty."

"MOM!"

The ploy to get his mother to change his bedtime, if clearly ineffective, will not be used with any frequency.

"I Want to Go Live at Dad's"

J.J. had had a bad evening. First his mother yelled at him for letting the dog out. Then she yelled at him for not putting the milk back in the refrigerator. And now she had just yelled at him because he was delaying his showering and getting ready for bed, and, in fact, she had come in and shut off the TV right in the middle of the program he was watching.

"I've had it with you, J.J. Get in there and take a shower."

J.J. started to cry. "I hate it here. I want to live at Dad's. I do."

The baby self is in action and it does not play fair. It can zero in on those areas in which the divorced parents are especially vulnerable: which parent is liked the best, who the child wants to live with, or even the effect of the divorce.

"Your divorce ruined my life," adds the still sobbing J.J.

My only point here, and it is a simple one, is that, as with all child complaints, one wants to be aware of *when* they are voiced. If they seem to appear only at times when the child is angry, has not gotten his or her way, and they do not appear at other times, then maybe those complaints do not mean a whole lot.

But what if he says it at other times when he really seems to have nothing to gain, when he is not mad at me?

Children do switch from staying with one parent to another and sometimes such a switch can be a good idea. But the change needs to be based on a full consideration of what seems best for them. Would they in truth be happier living with the other parent? However, that is a whole other and definitely very separate issue from J.J.'s getting yelled at for the umpteenth time for not picking up his room and then screaming, "I hate it here. I want to live at Dad's."

And maybe at his father's, if he is lucky, he won't have to pick up his room.

So Well-Behaved at My Ex's

It was six o'clock Sunday evening. Kevin and Judith were returning to their mother's from their every-other-weekend visit with their father. The children's parents had been divorced for four years. Their father's car was now pulling up in front to deliver the children. As they clambered out of the car, Kevin and Judith started yelling at each other.

"Stop it. Stop pushing."

"You stop it. Jerk!"

"Mom, Judith keeps pushing me."

They ran into the house past their mother who was standing at the door to greet them, continuing their screaming. As usual, their father came to the door to briefly report on the weekend.

"Kevin seems to still be coughing. I gave him the medicine. They were both very good. We had a good time. I'll be by Wednesday night at the usual time. Bye, Elizabeth."

"Bye, Ronald."

It was true that they had been very good at their father's, as they usually were. Yet, after *every* weekend at their father's, Kevin and Judith also usually kept screaming at each other for the rest of the evening.

"Mom! Mom! Tell him to stop."

A phenomenon well known to many divorced parents is the "being good at the weekend parent's house" syndrome. At least it's well known to the parent who has them most of the time. When they're at the other parent's house, the one who has them for a distinctly shorter period of time, they behave well. Sometimes, even siblings who cannot keep their hands off each other are on good behavior.

"No, Kevin and Judith get along well when they are with me."

But when they return to the more full-time parent, they instantly, and I do mean instantly, regress. They are particularly awful immediately upon return and often even into the next day. It can be maddening because it is easy to think:

I must be doing something wrong. After all, they're good for him, but not for me.

Or—

It has to be bad for them being at their father's, since I always get such bad fallout the day after they return.

But of course, it is a classic example of baby-self behavior. It can be a very frustrating phenomenon to behold, but very definitely it is *not* a sign that anything is wrong.

Frequently, the situation gets evened out a little. Let us say that Kevin and Judith's father were to have them for a sustained period of time—for example, a month in the summer. That is too long to sustain a mature self. Their baby selves would come out and they would start being awful. Their father, the less custodial parent, would get a dose of what their mother has been getting all along.

Single Parents

Suda, sitting by the fire with her children, looked up to see Og, her mate, enter the cave. Slung over his shoulder was the carcass of a batuk, a small antelopelike animal. Og threw the carcass on the cave floor.

"Nush da [Cook it]," said Og, and left the cave to join his comrades and discuss the day's hunt.

Suda got the meal ready while tending to the children.

Later Og returned for the meal, which included roast pala

(a wild cornlike vegetable). After the meal Og asked that his children be brought before him.

"Trandish tara fang graka samban [What today have you done of significance]?" he asked each child. To which they each gave a brief description of an event in their day. Og then dismissed his children and grabbed a gourd filled with faroo (an alcoholic beverage made from fermented lissa roots), from which he drank heavily. Og then fell asleep.

Og rose with the sun and headed out for another day of hunting. Suba went with other women of the village searching for edible plants and tubers. The children were left in the care of Og's mother, Lila Two Teeth.

Was Og much help in the raising of his children?

My point with the above story is that even though fathers have long been part of the home, they have traditionally not been especially involved in child raising. Most of that task has fallen to someone else, usually the mother. If there is help, it more usually comes from nonspouse relatives—grandparents or older siblings. In fact, the current trend in the United States, where more and more fathers are involved in day-to-day child care, is basically a new phenomenon, and it is wonderful for children. But de facto single parenting, typically by mothers, is not new.

Having two parents in the home is good for the parents and good for the kids. It is good for the parents because of the sharing. First, there can be sharing in child-care coverage, which can make child raising easier and less stressful. There can be sharing of responsibility. *I don't have to take full responsibility for all the decisions, for everything that happens with the kids. There is somebody else I can turn to.*

There also is shared experience, a special delight of two-parent families whose importance is not to be underestimated. *Jack's the only other person in the world who cares about the kids as I do, who's interested in them as much as I. Who else would actually care that Trisha, for the first time ever, brushed her teeth?*

Having two parents in the home is good for kids because a second parent can be a buffer. The second parent is an aid to prevent a child's becoming too engulfed in a relationship with the other parent. The second parent serves as a safety valve to insure enough normal, healthy distance and separation between parent and child.

But the main plus for children of having a second in-home parent is that it adds to the experience of childhood. The children build two very different relationships with two very different people. Each relationship gives the children different experiences of who they are, who the parents are, and of themselves within the relationships. Of course, when the two adults are of different sexes, the children also experience what relationships with different genders can be like.

Is it nicer for kids to have two at-home parents? I think the answer is definitely yes. But is it *necessary?* Can kids have a perfectly nice, even wonderful childhood, with a single parent? I think the answer to that is also yes.

Major problems do not come so much from which or how many adults are in the parenting role. Problems come where parents lack sufficient time, energy, patience, and flat-out availability to adequately provide for their children. That can be a problem especially where economic realities force parents to have less time with their children.

The family is what is important, but a family can have many forms: both parents, single parents, parent and step-parent, grandparents, even others. For a child, the actual makeup of the family is not what matters most. For a child, a family is people who are there and who can be counted on always to be there.

Lacking a Same-Sex Parent

But what about children who are raised without a same-sex parent in the home? Don't they need a same-sex role model with whom they can identify? Might it not make them more likely to become gay?

To the best of my knowledge, one's gender identity is not related to the gender of parents in the home. Beyond that, gender identity—how one goes about being a person of one's own sex, for better or for worse—is supplied more strongly by the culture at large than by the home. Friends, television, and what prevails as appropriate behavior for one's gender in the time and place that one lives are the biggest influences. Parents have a major influence, but the *kind* of gender model they provide is far more significant than the particular gender they model.

"I want to grow up to be like Daddy: strong—when Daddy says 'No' he means 'No'; loving—he cuddles me and always seems happy to be with me; considerate—he thinks of things that I care about even before I say them."

But perhaps having no model would be preferable to having the following:

"I want to grow up and be like Daddy—abusive to women, which he is to Mommy, and abusive to me when he is drunk."

"I want to grow up to be like Daddy and come home from work and watch television and fall asleep on the couch at eight o'clock."

Of course, models are not just for same-sex children.

"I want to grow up to marry somebody like Daddy who listens to me, cares about me, and always takes the time to be with me."

Divorce as a Change of Circumstance

One of the major effects on children of separation and divorce comes from changes that are often not for the better. Children may have to move to a different house with the parent who has left. With a move comes, almost certainly, a change of neighborhoods and loss of friends. Children may have to change schools, and starting in a new school entails many more changes. The bottom line is that they lose what they had and are forced to start anew. There are some children who seem to be able to handle all these changes—making a fresh start without too much trouble. But for some the changes can be a real problem.

Another very real change that comes with divorce is that there is less money. Two households now must exist on the same money that had previously supported one. For many families this can mean a true notch downward in what they can afford. Suddenly much that was assumed is no longer available.

> *"Why can't we go to McDonald's anymore?"*
> *"Why can't I get new sneakers?"*
> *"We're poor now, aren't we?"*
> *"No, but we do have to watch what we spend more than we did when your Mom and I were together."*

Again, for some children this is not a major problem. But for others—especially the worriers—it can be. They start worrying a lot about money where previously they hadn't given it a thought.

Another change that can come with a divorce is that a previously happy, or at least emotionally stable, parent can be transformed into one who is extremely upset and who may never, unfortunately, get it back together. The child now has a parent who is more upset, more emotionally vulnerable, less effective as a parent and therefore more for a child to worry about. The unfortunate effect on children is that often they will push the weakened parent harder, especially if he or she is the main custodial parent. Rather than backing off in the face of a troubled parent, they constantly push in the vain hope of getting the strength that was there before and that they now sorely miss. Or, in the absence of a strong caregiver, turn into a parentified child—becoming caregivers themselves— and losing out on much of their childhood.

Last, and most important, can come the significant loss of a parent—most often the father—who previously, for better or for worse, was in the home, was interacted with regularly, and was an ongoing and significant part of one's life. With the divorce, this parent can become less and less available until, as especially can happen when one or the other parent moves a sizable distance away, he (usually) is no longer very present in one's life.

I mean I still have a father and I love him. But I don't get to see him at all except two weeks in the summer. And phone calls. But those aren't a lot.

All of the above are real and potentially damaging issues for children that can come with a divorce. Not all of them bear resolution. There is no way around them. They are just the consequences of the divorce and sometimes not for better, but for worse.

Loss of Stability

But certain other possible long-term results of divorce may not be as problematic for children as they seem. Although the original structure of the home is now lost and the children face a period of readjustment, a sense of stability is not necessarily gone from their lives. There may be many changes,

including shifting constellations in the specifics of a life—
Mommy's new boyfriend, new step-siblings, a new city to live
in, spending big chunks of time in two different places—but
most important to them is whether the sun in their universe
remains in place. Are the person or persons they count on the
most still there? Will they keep being there? And if the answer
is yes, they have the most important stability of all.

In families where both parents have been an integral part
of a child's life, following a divorce such children often continue to have substantial ongoing contact with both parents.
Usually they live with one parent but visit regularly with the
other and often have phone contact in between. Usually these
children who grow up with two parents they see regularly come
to accept their situation as a normal and perfectly workable
arrangement.

Five years later:

"I live at Mom's, but go over to Dad's most weekends and
I see him pretty much whenever I want."

Which place do you like better?

"I don't know. I like it both places."

Do you want it to be any different?

"No, not really."

Do you wish your parents would get back together?

"Yeah."

Do you think they will?

"No."

Do you think about it much?

"Not really. I like it the way it is."

The Long-Term Effect on Relationships

Finally, what effect does divorce have on children's long-term ability to form stable and lasting adult relationships? Does their childhood experience of a failed relationship between their parents undermine their future ability or willingness to make strong, permanent adult relationships of their own?

There is disagreement about this. My opinion is rather simple and falls within the framework of what has already been discussed in these pages.

There is no question that experiencing divorce has an influence on a child's later relationships. But I also think that far and away the greatest factor in what shapes the ability and wish to make strong, long-term relationships in adult life is not the nature of one's parents' relationship with each other, but the nature of *one's own* relationship with one's parents.

If those child and parent relationships are bad because both parents are harsh, selfish, controlling, unloving, or giving love only conditionally, then one is going to look upon love relationships as having the potential for all of the above, and be untrustful of such relationships. Furthermore, because one was the recipient of defective love, which has become part of oneself, it becomes harder to give the kind of love and tolerance necessary for successful long-term relationships.

But if a child is not abandoned and if throughout the childhood there continues to be a consistent, *unconditionally* loving parent or parents, then that fact above all else is going to produce inside the child and the future adult the ability and the wish to reproduce such a relationship. Having been loved in that way, one wants and trusts that one can get it and return it.

6

Problems That May

Not Be Problems

One piece of good news about child raising is that there are many issues parents spend much time and energy being concerned about that they really do not have to. Most of these issues arise when parents attach excessive importance to ordinary events.

"If I say yes to a toy that he wants even though he has just gotten another toy, aren't I creating a spoiled child?"

"If I don't stamp out her lying now—she has just lied about how all the sand got into the kitchen—won't she become a dishonest person?"

"If his play with his action figures is very violent, shouldn't I be concerned that he will grow into a violent person?"

This section is about a number of those issues—as they arise in our day-to-day dealings with our children—where there may not be as much at stake as we might think.

Spoiled Children

Parents frequently worry about somehow spoiling their children. They do not want to do anything that might end up producing a "spoiled child." But in regard to what actually makes for spoiled children, much that parents worry about is groundless.

We all can describe spoiled children. They are never satisfied and always want and expect more than is their right. They want everything done for them, want everything to come to them, but never want to expend the least bit of energy on their own. Moreover, they assume that that is the way that it is supposed to be.

"Mommy."

"What is it, Egbert?"

"Would you please bring me a peanut butter sandwich with the edges cut off and with two jelly crisscrosses not quite touching the edges," says thirty-six-year-old Egbert reclining on his pillows watching his two televisions.

"Certainly, Egbert," says his mother.

"Remember, be careful that the jelly crisscrosses don't touch the edges. One of them did last time."

"I know. I'm sorry, Egbert. I will try to do better," says his mother, wincing with each step because of her bad arthritis as she heads to the kitchen.

Spoiling can last a lifetime, as in Egbert's case, but it's a fact of child development that spoiling does not come from giving or from saying yes.

In a store, Kyle's father happened to notice two particularly evil-looking action figures, Lizardus and Tenagra, which he thought Kyle would love to have. Kyle's father wanted to buy them on the spot and give them to Kyle when he got home that evening. But only last week he bought him two other action figures, and Kyle already had a *very* large collection that he treasured and played with endlessly. Kyle certainly did not *need* any more action figures. Kyle's father was afraid that giving Kyle two more would spoil him. Perhaps he could buy them now and give them to Kyle at another time. However, Kyle's father didn't want to wait. He wanted to give them to Kyle that day. He could picture how excited Kyle would be by the two new monster men.

Giving is always good. We cannot give too much. In the course of normal child raising, we supply plenty of noes. We never have to say no for fear that we have said yes too much. Character is not built from saying no on principle, saying no for the sake of it. Life supplies plenty of noes and will take care of that.

Spoiling, as is easily recognizable with thirty-six-year-old Egbert, comes from altogether different sources. Spoiling comes from failing to make appropriate demands: "No, I am not going to tie your shoelaces for you. You know how to do it." Above all, spoiling comes from allowing oneself to be bullied by the baby self into doing what one does not want to do.

"But Egbert, you know it's hard for me to have to go back into the kitchen again."

"I'm holding my breath. I won't breathe unless you clean off some of the jelly. I'm not breathing. Starting now."

"Oh, all right, dear."

Grandparents Who Spoil

"Whenever the kids stay at Nana and Papa's they're spoiled rotten. Their grandparents let them do anything. The kids can get away with everything and then expect the same deal when they get home."

No, they do not. They will try, but if they know that the

rules are different at home than at Nana and Papa's, and if parents assert their rules, they do not try very hard. This is a great example of different rules for different places.

If children have in their life an occasional place of constant delights and *no* appropriate demands, and if that place is a sometimes-place, isn't that a nice thing for them? Isn't it something special that they will always look back on with great fondness? Besides, unless grandparents are the major caregivers, their input is not what will shape a child, nor will their spoiling cause problems or character flaws.

Lying

Susan, the mother of Sam, Bobo, and Tracy, came into the kitchen and noticed a large puddle of orange juice in front of the refrigerator. Because Sam and Tracy had been within Susan's sight since the last time she was in the kitchen, she knew that it was Bobo's mess.

"Bobo! Bobo!"

"What?" said Bobo, coming into the kitchen.

"Did you spill the orange juice?"

"No," said Bobo.

"Bobo, I know it was you. Tracy and Sam have been with me."

"It wasn't me. I didn't spill the orange juice."

"Don't lie to me, Bobo."

"I'm not lying. Somebody else did it. I don't know who. I didn't do it, Mom. Honest." Bobo, who was lying through his teeth, sounded very sincere.

"Now I am going to give you one more chance, Bobo. I want you to tell me the truth. Did you spill the orange juice?"

"No, Mom. I didn't. I don't know how it got spilled."

"I know you're lying, Bobo."

"I'm not, Mom. I'm not. I'm not lying."

"Bobo, it is one thing to spill the orange juice and leave it there—"

"I didn't, Mom."

"But now you're lying. And you just keep lying. I'll give you one more chance and then you're in big trouble."

"What happens if I did spill it and now I tell you? Not that I did."

"I don't know, Bobo. You've already been lying so much I'm disgusted."

"Okay, I did spill it. It was an accident and I didn't notice that it was a big spill."

"You're still lying. You did notice. You were just too lazy to clean it up."

"No, Mom. I didn't see that it made a big puddle."

"You just don't stop lying, do you? Get to your room, Bobo. No TV tonight."

"But Mom, it was an accident. I didn't notice it made a mess."

"Get out of here, Bobo."

"You're not fair. You never believe me."

"I will if you start telling the truth."

"I do tell the truth."

"Get out of here, Bobo."

Children lie, and they do it much more often than not when confronted with a possible crime.

"Jason, was it you who left the water running in the sink?"

"No."

"Anna Lee, did you wash your hands?"

"Yes."

"Sissy, did you eat all the chocolate macadamia nut cookies?"

"I just ate one."

• • •

Children often lie even when there is nothing that they are going to be blamed for. To trigger lying, children only need to perceive the *slightest* possibility of blame.

"Sondra, were you just in your room?"

"No." But she was.

"Oh, I just wondered if I left my knitting in there."

"Oh. No, it's not in my room."

What had Sondra been afraid of being blamed for? Even she was not sure. It was just the phrasing of the question that made her wary.

Children lie where it is bizarrely obvious that they are guilty.

"Holden, did you take Nicholas's purple troll?"

"No." He's holding it in his right hand.

"What is that?"

"I don't know."

That children lie is neither bad nor good. They do it as an immediate way of deflecting blame. Children do not like to be blamed. It does not seem to matter whether parents are harsh and nasty or loving and gentle. The fear of blame seems universally lodged in children's heads—inevitable as the dark side of their developing conscience. The angry face of blame.

"Oh, you are in trouble now. *Big* trouble."

And to escape, they lie. For as children they are still too young to stand up to that angry nemesis. They simply do not yet have the psychological strength. Many of us do not have it even later.

Being wholly honest is not easy.

"Sissy, did you eat all the chocolate macadamia nut cookies?"

"Yes, I did. I know I wasn't supposed to. But they were just so good I couldn't stop myself. So I ate them all."

That is not an answer that children give. It is the exact truth. But such an answer leaves them feeling open to intolerable blame. In her head, she winces at her mother's imagined, blaming voice.

"Sissy, how could you? What a terrible, piggy thing to do!"

She cannot admit it so openly. No child can.

So what should parents do about lying?

"Bobo! Bobo!"

"What?" said Bobo, coming into the kitchen.

"Bobo, would you please clean up this orange juice?"

"I didn't spill it."

"Bobo, would you please clean up the orange juice?" No mention of Bobo's denial. "When you spill something, it is not good to leave it. Somebody might slip on it, or maybe step in it, and track it all over the house."

"But I didn't spill it."

"Bobo, clean up the orange juice."

Maybe Bobo's mother can get Bobo to clean up the orange juice and maybe she cannot. But it is the cleanup, not the lying, on which Bobo's mother is choosing to focus. Parents have a choice. They can focus on the lying, or they can focus on the issue at hand. I recommend the latter course.

"Jason, was it you who left the water running in the sink?"

"No."

"I had to turn it off. It wastes water. Try to remember to turn it off after you use the sink."

"Anna Lee, did you wash your hands?"

"Yes."

"I don't think so. Go in and wash them. Now!"

"Sissy, did you eat all the chocolate macadamia nut cookies?"

"I just ate one."

"Sissy, I told you not to eat all the cookies. I asked you not to. Now that makes me very angry. I just don't think I can trust leaving bags of cookies around anymore."

This is clean, simple, and stays on the subject. In the end, it is not very useful to make an issue of the lying.

"I Want Him to Tell the Truth about What He Did"

One problem with my approach to lying is that it puts the responsibility on the parent for deciding what actually happened. Obviously, this opens up the possibility that the parent may occasionally falsely accuse the child of a misdeed. But this is one of the places where not using punishment has a distinct advantage. For without punishment, the worst that can happen to a child is that he or she will have to do things like clean up somebody else's mess, or unjustly feel their parent's ire.

"But I didn't, Mom."

"I don't want to hear about it, Justin."

"But I DIDN'T!"

"Get out of here!"

Justin *will* be outraged, infuriated, and upset. But how bad is it to be occasionally falsely accused of something when one is not punished for it and overall knows that one's parents are loving and do try to be fair?

The alternative—parent in the role of interrogator—is far worse. If a parent makes a big deal about lying, then it becomes important that he or she determine in each instance whether the child is lying or not. The parent is forced to bring in the heavy guns and truly ghastly scenes can be created in the pursuit of finding out the truth. It can become a major mistake.

"I want you to tell me, Sissy. *Did you make that mess out in the garage?*"

"No, Mom, I swear to God."

"Sissy, you had better not be lying. I want to know the truth. Did you make that mess?"

"No, Mom, I didn't. I didn't."

Instead, just as Bobo's mother did, parents should make their best guess based on their available knowledge of the accused and of the circumstances. If they think their child is lying, proceed as just described.

Spilled Orange Juice or Lying?

But perhaps the major problem with focusing on lying—as illustrated in the example with Bobo—is that it gets off the subject and away from the problem at hand. In the case with Bobo, the spilled orange juice has been forgotten. A far more momentous issue has been raised: the teaching of honesty and the correction of character flaws. This switch is another major mistake in child raising.

If you are tempted to focus on the lying, remember that the presence of nasty character traits in children does not mean a whole lot. Lying is baby-self behavior. It is not indicative of any future flaws. Baby selves, if sensing the slightest chance of blame, will *always* lie. In fact, lying in childhood, but especially at home and with parents, has little if anything to do with becoming an honest person.

Let me give a last example.

James Earl mistakenly got into his head that his mother would not let him take his fancy box of Magic Markers over to his friend Bennett's house. (She had once said something about not carrying the box all over the place because he could lose them.) Consequently, James Earl made up an elaborate story about how Bennett's mother had specifically requested that James Earl bring over the Magic Markers because *she* wanted to see them.

But the story rang false to adult ears.

"James Earl, none of that's true. Mrs. Wilson said no such thing."

"She did, Mom."

"You don't have to lie. It's fine with me if you take the Magic Markers over to Bennett's. I know how much you like them and how much you like other people to see them. It's fine with me."

"It is?"

"Yes."

"Oh."

Isn't James Earl's mother making a mistake? Isn't she rewarding the lying? Isn't she giving James Earl the message "You can get away with lying"?

That actually is not the message at all. The message that James Earl's mother is giving is that whether you lie or not is irrelevant to what I decide. I will make my decisions, as I always do, based on my judgment of what I want for you and what I think is best for you. Your behavior does not control my decisions. With me you can lie or not lie because, as part of your childhood, it just does not matter. Out there, separate from me, it does matter. And there you will have to take your chances. I cannot protect you from the consequences of your behavior out there. But with me, my gift to you—your childhood—is that what you do does not matter.

This is, as always, the wonderful deal.

Teaching Honesty

But you can't just ignore the lying. Lying is bad. Aren't parents supposed to teach their children not to lie? How will children learn not to lie? How will they learn to be honest?

Yes, we do want to teach our children not to lie and to grow up to be honest. So how *do* we produce children who grow up to be honest?

1. Deal with your child honestly. Nothing could be more important.
2. Act honestly in your dealings with others, as an example for your child.
3. Nurture your child.
4. Set limits and make appropriate demands in the course of child raising.
5. Do not act toward your child in an overly harsh manner.

The last three recommendations would seem to have little to do with honesty. But they do, because to be honest you have to be able to own up to your mistakes, and you have to trust that you can survive in the world without having to be dishonest. To do both of the these, you have to feel good about yourself and your ability to survive in the world. The last three recommendations produce that confidence.

Noticeably absent from this list is telling one's child that lying is bad. Actually, that does have some effect, but its role is really minor. As any parent who has raised a child knows, castigating and perhaps punishing one's child for lying has zero effect on whether the child will or will not lie again. In fact, the main effect of making a very big deal about it or punishing someone for it is that children become extra careful about not being caught in lies. Plus, it makes for horrible scenes.

Storytelling

Nate's mother overheard her son talking to his friend Danny.

"So last weekend we went to visit my grandfather. He is

very rich. He lives in a mansion and he has lots of horses and whenever we go there, I get to ride his horses. If you don't believe me, see this bruise on my arm? That's how I got the bruise. Falling off one of his horses. I'm not a very good horse rider yet, but I'm getting to be."

None of the above contained a word of truth.

Storytelling is an altogether different species from lying. Lying is to escape blame. But storytelling is to paint a better picture. "We have six dogs, you know." It's to gain respect or notoriety in the eyes of others. "I found a twenty-dollar bill lying on the ground yesterday. Just lying there."

What Nate's parents should do about storytelling is generally nothing. They should not interfere if the story is told to a friend. That's between Nate and his friends. As he gets older, they will increasingly doubt him. "You're full of bull, Nate." Experience teaches Nate to curb his storytelling.

But there *can* be problems with storytelling.

Alex to his father:

"There's this kid in school, Jamie. Well, he keeps picking on me and Mrs. Jenkins doesn't do anything about it. And during recess he kicked me for no reason. So me and him got into a big fight. And I kicked his butt."

Alex continues to tell his father a sequence of similar stories of Jamie picking on him, other fights with him, and Mrs. Jenkins doing nothing. His stories finally prompted his father to call Mrs. Jenkins.

"No, Alex and Jamie haven't been in any fights. They get along fine. No, I have no idea why Alex would say what he did."

Alex's father might be able to figure out why Alex told the stories or he might not. However, Alex's father definitely does not want to continue to make embarrassing phone calls to school over incidents that never happened.

"Alex, I called Mrs. Jenkins today because I was worried about your continual fighting with Jamie. She says you don't fight. I do not like calling Mrs. Jenkins because I'm worried about you and finding out that nothing is wrong."

In this example, Alex's father has clearly told his son that storytelling can have unintended consequences, so you have to watch what you say. There's nothing more he can do. Is extensive storytelling in childhood a warning sign that a child might lack confidence? Perhaps, which is why parents should be watchful if there are other signs that their child might lack confidence. But the bottom line really is that storytelling, even a great deal of storytelling, falls well within the norms of childhood. It is something that most do outgrow. Which means that what parents should basically do about storytelling is not worry about it.

Talking Back

"No, Aaron, the TV goes off now and no more fussing."
"You're the one that's fussing."

Back talk. Ultimately there are two basic facts about back talk. The first has to do with the baby self.

Back talk comes from the baby self. It is the baby self talking. As discussed repeatedly in these pages, the baby self feeds on parent response—any kind of parent response. And because the baby self eats parent response, any kind of immediate parent response to back talk other than harsh punishment or hard smacks across the face will only tend to increase back talk, not reduce it. Hence, angry rebukes—"You better watch your mouth"—or threats of punishment—"That's it. You're going to bed half an hour earlier"—will not diminish back talk.

Fact #1: If parents' aim is to reduce back talk to a minimum, the most effective immediate response—again short of harsh punishment or hard smacks—is nonresponse.

"No, Aaron, the TV goes off now and no more whining/
fussing."

"You're the one that's whining."

"Turn off the TV."

Later, if you want, but only later:

"Aaron, I do not like your back talk. I asked you to turn off
the TV and I do not like you talking back."

And having made your point no more need be said.

Fact #2: Parents who do not use harsh punishment or hard
smacks across the face as part of child-raising practice *are*
allowing back talk. It is a choice. But allowing and approving
are not the same thing. Parents may actively disapprove of
back talk—a message their children *will* hear.

Getting in the Last Word

"I don't want you touching my nail polish, and that's it."
"But I won't make a mess."
"No, we've been through this before. No."
"But it's not fair."
"No, Carly, that is it."
"No, it's not. You never listen to me."
"Carly, drop it!"
"You're mean. You are."
"You better watch it, Carly."
"You better watch it."

Children like to get in the last word. We like to get in the
last word. Strategically, from a parent's standpoint, entering
into a "who gets the last word" battle usually does not work
out well. But strategic considerations aside, we as parents have
to decide which is the more adult thing to do: to get in the
last word, or to let them. It's our choice.

Aggressive Behavior

At her preschool, four-year-old Tanya saw that Stephen was playing with some new blocks. She decided that she wanted to play with them, so she went over and, without saying anything, started taking the blocks away from Stephen.

"Stop," said Stephen, trying to hold onto the blocks.

"No," said Tanya, and she slugged Stephen pretty hard on his arm. Stephen started to cry.

Aggressive behavior. Not nice. But maybe not always as bad as it seems.

Violence—intentionally causing harm to another—is always bad. Yet aggression—forceful action aimed at another —is not always the same as violence. Aggression is hitting somebody hard in the face. But it is also hitting a baseball as hard as one can. Aggression is maliciously teasing a classmate about an ugly birthmark. But it is also calling out to a waitress to take one's order in a crowded restaurant where one has been ignored for twenty minutes. Aggression is grabbing a toy from another child without asking. But it is also going back again to try to solve a frustrating math problem and actually fighting through the frustration in search of a solution. Aggression is a normal, healthy, and necessary part of our psychological makeup. In fact, aggression—directed productively—is a necessary part of achieving, of getting what one wants, and hence a necessary part of a successful and happy life. Aggressive behavior is not bad.

Aggressive behavior that harms others is bad. The task for parents is not to quash aggressive behavior, but to draw the line where it may become harmful. Parents must always seek to prevent aggressive behavior that could cause serious harm, such as a sibling pushed hard while coming down the stairs, or a rock thrown during a play fight. The message must be: Behavior that can cause serious harm to yourself or others will not be allowed. But parents want to be wary of giving the message that all aggressive behavior is bad.

Seven-year-old Stephanie was playing Lot-O-Squares with her friend Sophie, but she became frustrated because she was losing and punched Sophie in the back.

"You're cheating."

Sophie immediately punched Stephanie back and they started fighting.

Stephanie's mother, who was sitting in the same room, immediately intervened.

"Girls, stop. It's not nice. If the two of you can't play without fighting, then Sophie is going to have to go home."

I give the above example because parents seem to be more likely to inhibit aggressive behavior in girls, specifically to promote the idea that aggressive behavior is unseemly for girls, that it *looks* bad. It is not what little girls do. But parents should be careful that this message does not come across *more effectively* than they might wish. Aggressive behavior in boys *or* in girls is not bad.

Aggressive Play and Fantasy

Perhaps the most misunderstood issue in regard to aggression and violence is the relationship between aggressive and violent play and fantasy and real violence. The pretend versus the real.

Six-year-old Lawrence was outside having a good time. His mother, reading a magazine, was seated in a lawn chair nearby. Lawrence had found a number of sticks and placed them in the ground so that they made a small grouping of upright twigs.

"This is the Army of the Kraxer," said Lawrence. "Everybody's scared of them."

Lawrence then got up and went over to his big plastic Whirlycycle.

"But not Lawrence Man."

And Lawrence proceeded to ride his Whirlycycle over the grouping of standing twigs. Flattening them.

"They're all pancakes," said Lawrence laughing.

Lawrence then again methodically set up the twigs all over again.

"No. Please. Save us. We won't hurt you," said Lawrence in a funny high voice.

"I don't think so," said Lawrence in his normal voice as again the Whirlycycle flattened the standing army of twigs.

"Mushed people pancakes," said Lawrence, laughing.

Lawrence repeated this performance a number of times. But finally he grew bored of this particular game.

"Please. No. Please," said Lawrence in his high funny voice as he stood over the once-again-flattened twigs.

"Now you die," said Lawrence and started stomping the twigs. "Die. Die," he said as he stomped until they were finally imbedded in the earth.

Lawrence's mother watched this violent performance by her son. She was concerned. *What is wrong with him?*

The answer is that nothing is wrong with Lawrence. Early in life children come to learn that there is a whole realm where what goes on does not really happen. It is a world of pretend, of fantasy. In this realm anything can happen and yet it does not happen "for real."

It is a very important realm because nasty thoughts and feelings that if acted on in the real world would be a serious problem indeed can be expressed in a totally harmless way and can even feel good. In fact, people who can make use of fantasy are actually less, not more, likely to act out angry feelings. The world of pretend supplies a healthy outlet for feelings that might otherwise stay bottled up inside, growing, with nowhere to go, no place to be expressed, except through direct action.

We can relieve all kinds of emotions through fantasy. We do it as adults.

"I just hate my boss. I would truly like to strangle him sometimes. I mean it."

"I know what you mean. I always want to strangle Howard. Maybe I'll do it next Thursday."

Both women know that neither is actually going to do anything. But it does feel good to think about it anyway.

Some children can be particularly expressive in their fantasies. Usually this means that these children have a more dramatic flair and richer imaginations. It does not mean that they are more likely to do what they express, though their productions can be disconcerting.

"Jamie drew a picture in school of a man with thirteen arrows sticking out of him. And drops of blood coming out." This drawing was probably the envy of his classmates. "I do worry about him."

Wishing, expressing, and fantasizing about nasty things are not a problem. They are very normal. Can fantasy *cause* potentially harmful actions? There is no question that fantasy can give form to such actions. But it is *not* fantasy that promotes violence. Violence does not come from violent fantasies. Fantasy may give form to the violence, but violence comes from anger and poor impulse control. Both of those, as repeatedly stated here, more than anything else, come from having been dealt with violently and without restraint. Overall, the use of fantasy is an inhibitor of violence, not a cause.

What Causes Violence in Children—What Parents Can Do

Seven-year-old Lyle's father happened to be passing through the TV room where his children were watching television.

"You're gonna die like you and all of your kind," said the

man on television holding a gun, which he then fired four times at another man, who then fell, presumably dead.

Lyle's father went over and turned off the TV.

"Lyle, I thought you were supposed to be watching cartoons."

"I got bored," said Lyle.

"You know you're not allowed to watch that stuff."

"Yeah," said Lyle.

Later that day, Lyle was playing outside with Clark, a boy his age who lived two houses away.

"You're gonna die like you and all of your kind," said Lyle as he pointed a stick at his friend. "Kh . . . kh . . . kh," said Lyle and then, throwing down the stick, he ran as fast as he could at Clark, slamming into him and knocking him to the ground.

"You're dead," said Lyle.

Certainly the violence in our world, including the representations of that world that reach into our homes, especially through television, has an influence on our children. Seeing violence on TV can be scary and/or stimulating to a young mind, especially if the violence is depicted as cool, funny, something to be emulated. Yet these images fall into relative insignificance compared to what is most important, what we as parents do with our children.

If we want to raise children who will not become part of the violence in our world, we cannot be violent with our children. If we are loving and considerate and not violent with our children, if we can practice self-control, then we have gone very far toward insuring that they will not be a part of that violence, regardless of what the world may throw at them.

One exception is when children are raised in an environment of misery and desperation, where their day-to-day safety truly is in question, and where they see no hope in their future.

In these cases, many of the stays against violence are removed and the influences of the home, though still powerful, can lose out to a world whose harsh reality transcends anything that we as parents can protect them from.

Competition

The idea of competition is that you aggressively try to beat people. You win. They lose. Is competition aggressiveness channeled into healthy goals? Or is it just another way in which aggressive people learn to get what they want at the expense of others?

Eight-year-old Jimmy had his friend Brian over to his house and they were playing a game of checkers. Jimmy lost and had a fit. He turned bright red and started to yell, "I'm never going to play with you again. I hate checkers." His behavior went more or less downhill from there. His friend Brian sat and watched.

Jimmy's father, who was also observing this scene, was appalled by the behavior of his son. *Jimmy just can't deal with losing. It's terrible.*

Later, Jimmy's father gave him a talk about how he was wrong to care so much about winning, that the point of games was to have fun, not to win.

"But I *want* to win," said Jimmy.

Is competition—trying to win for the sake of winning—bad for children?

The criticism of competition, of those truly competitive situations where there is clearly a winner and a loser, is:

(1) If children lose, their spirits are crushed, their self-esteem potentially damaged.

Or, perhaps worse, (2) they develop a winning-is-everything attitude, where all they care about is winning and in the process they grow insensitive to the feelings and needs of others; competitiveness and sensitivity to others become incompatible.

Competition at its best, in checkers, in baseball, in horse-back riding, in school, is to be able to try your hardest, to extend yourself to the fullest, and to do your best, within a framework where you will be challenged. It's a strong motivator, and children who achieve tend to be very competitive. But competition includes winning and losing.

Young children do not take the losing part of competition particularly gracefully. But as they get older, many children learn to control their tempers when they lose and change their perspective about winning and losing.

"I do want to win. As much as I ever did. But it's not everything. I can have fun if I lose. Though it does make me mad. But it also challenges me to want to go out and try again."

Children learn to compete against themselves.

"It was great. I came in third—which is about what I usually do—but I did my best time ever."

"I lost as usual to Rodney, but it was six-four, seven-five. I'm really getting into a groove of hitting the ball well."

None of this is incompatible with caring about others. If a child is evolving as a caring person, competition gets put into that context. It is fun to strive and to win, but I also want opponents who can stand up to me. I do not want to win at all costs, suffering caused to others be damned.

Adults, of course, can pervert competition for children, saying that the point *is* to win, rather than to have fun and to achieve one's best. Losing is unacceptable. Losing is for losers.

Sometimes competitions end on a positive note. Everybody congratulates everybody else for having participated to the fullest, and that is where the honor is. Trying. The disaster is where the losers are somehow seen as less good, less honorable.

But healthy competition—and there *is* such a thing—can definitely enrich a life.

One summer day, when my Nick was about ten, I was in our backyard doing some sort of yard work. Nick was playing basketball with two friends in the driveway, our makeshift court. As I worked in the back, I could hear their basketball game—not the sound of bouncing ball, or ball off rim or backboard, but loud arguing and much swearing. Occasionally I would come to the other side of the house to watch, and rarely was there actual basketball being played. Mainly there was more arguing and swearing. Was the ball out of bounds? Was it a foul? Did he double dribble? In fact, over the course of an hour, there may have been five minutes of actual playing.

But the arguing was part of the game, too. As anybody who plays knows, an essential part of basketball is the establishment of agreed-upon rules so that the game may continue unimpeded. What is out of bounds? What constitutes traveling? How much aggressiveness (fouling) will or will not be permitted? As a teenager or an adult, if one is to play basketball, especially in informal playground pickup games where there is no referee, one has to know and be able to play with already agreed-upon rules, without having to renegotiate, so that the game can go on and be fun.

The knowledge of these rules and the ability to play by them does not magically spring fully developed from nowhere. These skills are thrashed out over many, many childhood basketball games, just in the manner Nick and his friends were doing.

As a young adult, Nick loves to play basketball, and he plays a lot. But in fact, some people do not have the temperament for the flat-out competitiveness and the inevitable arguing that accompany the game, and they ultimately back off from basketball. Or they develop a less serious, more nonchalant style of playing that allows them to play in a less emotion-laden manner. But invariably they do not enjoy the game as much as the more competitive types.

What is my point? That there are real benefits in life to participating, trying, hanging in there. But trying has built into it times of frustration and disappointment—which do hurt. Yet the rewards are substantial. Parents do well to encourage and to sustain such efforts. And if parents emphasize trying and persistence—not victories—the benefits for their children can be considerable.

7

More Difficult Problems

Accepting Too Well

Not being aggressive enough can be a serious problem. It's a more subtle issue than being too aggressive but nonetheless pernicious. If I care too much about what "they" will think, if I worry too much about the consequences of my actions, I can as a result inhibit the good normal aggressive parts of my personality, I can end up playing it too safe and become, ultimately, too indecisive and unable to act. Unfortunately, I can end up playing into one of the baby self's more insidious and crippling schemes (as discussed in Chapter 1).

"Mommy, can I have another snack tart?"

"No, Jessica. It's too close to supper."

"Please, Mommy. I'm really hungry."

"I said 'No,' Jessica."

And Jessica sighs, casts down her eyes, turns and dejectedly leaves the kitchen. Alone, Jessica feels bad about not getting the snack tart. She had really wanted it.

"I never get what I want. Never, ever."

After a little while and a few tears, Jessica feels fine again.

Without making a big fuss, Jessica had accepted her mother's refusal of another snack tart, felt sad for a while, but then it was over. Unlike her brother Malcolm, who always had huge fits at the drop of a hat, and who was the bane of their parents' existence even though they loved him dearly.

"Why couldn't he at least sometimes be a little more like Jessica?"

We want to be able to accept disappointment. Yet Jessica really had wanted the additional snack tart. In fact, she had wanted it just as much as her brother had in a similar situation only a couple of days earlier, when he had had one of his typical major fits. Jessica had been just as disappointed. It was just that she, unlike Malcolm, did not put up a huge hassle to try to get her mother to change her mind. However, Malcolm's tantrum had *not* gotten him another snack tart, either.

Underneath acceptance, underneath nonaggressiveness, the baby self can lurk in its passive guise. In this guise, it abhors aggressive behavior because aggressive behavior takes chances—you might get hurt, people might not like you. The baby self in its passive guise always wants to play it safe. But when we heed its wishes we can become unwilling and ultimately unable to take responsibility for what happens to us and are no longer effective actors in our own lives. We feel our fates are not in our own hands. We develop a philosophical sadness, a resignation; we believe things in the world do not seem to go our way and that there is little that we can do about it. Our lives are very much in the hands of the big world and that world can often be unkind. In effect, we may become victims, and we truly believe that there is no other way. We minimize the roles we can play in our own lives.

But what can I do? The world is very big and powerful and I am small and powerless. My life is shaped by others. And I must accept this because it is the way of the world.

An especially insidious part of dealing with life in this way is that it has one huge advantage. That advantage is that—even though I may suffer, feel depressed, even very depressed—I am free from the responsibility for my own life and from all of the *anxieties* of making decisions. Many people will take depression over anxiety every time. Depression may hurt, but it can still be somehow comfortable. Anxiety never is. I have handed the responsibility for myself over to others, to fate, which is so much more powerful than little ineffective me.

In children, the baby self in its passive guise likes to latch onto Mommy and put everything into her hands. (I described this earlier.) The passive baby self, who readily turns the responsibility for *everything* over to others, makes it difficult for parents to stay out of decisions a child needs to make.

"What kind of ice cream would you like, dear?"

"I don't know, you decide, Mommy. You know what I like."

But these same children, in the long run, may deprive themselves of the decision-making ability necessary to exist on their own.

All that decision making, all that responsibility, is just too stressful.

The ability to accept disappointment is a crucial part of maturity. But too much acceptance, total abnegation of one's role as a significant player in one's own life, is not maturity at all. First, there is a relationship between normal healthy aggressiveness and risk taking. They go together, which is why we as parents want to be careful that we do not inhibit normal aggressiveness. Second, parents need be aware that the baby self can take this passive route. Consequently, we want to make sure that we do not inadvertently remove all the risk taking from our children's lives. It is easy to make decisions for our children, especially if they seem so unsure and genuinely want us to do it for them. Many decisions are appropriately in our domain. But many decisions they must make for themselves.

"Mommy, should I wear my frilly shirt today or my red one?"
"That's up to you, Lila."
"But I don't know which."
"I guess you'll just have to decide."
"But I can't."
"I don't know what to tell you, Lila."
"Tell me which."
"I'm sorry, Lila. It's your choice."
"But I can't choose. You have to."
"Don't be late for breakfast. I have to get my stuff ready for work."
"I won't go to school."
"No, that's not an option."
"I won't."
Silence.
"Which is better? You have to tell me."

But her mother wasn't even in the room anymore.

Lila really *did* want to go to school. She did not at all like missing school, and really had no intention of not going. But also, Lila really could not decide which shirt to wear. She was growing progressively more agitated.

"WHICH?" she screamed at her mother.

Lila started pacing her room. "Which?" she again screamed.

"Almost time for the bus," called Lila's mother.

Now desperate, actually sweating, though it was cold in her room, Lila grabbed the frilly shirt and put it on. She then ran downstairs and yelled at her mother.

"You didn't help me. It doesn't look good. Everybody is gonna hate me."

But Lila did make her decision. In doing so, she ends up the winner, whatever she decided. Despite her trepidation, her fear of having made a wrong decision, she did decide. Just that decision, that small piece of being an aggressive, forceful player in her own life, makes her feel bigger, stronger, better. And of course everybody at her school thought that the frilly shirt looked just fine.

Painful Problems in Their Lives

Eight-year-old Jackie came home from school crying. As she sobbed, she told her mother that Debbie Prokowski, who disliked her, had invited everybody in the class to her birthday party, but had intentionally excluded Jackie.

Jackie was heartbroken.

That night, when her mother was putting her to bed, Jackie again began to cry.

"Nobody likes me. I hate school. I hate Debbie Prokowski. Why does this always happen to me?" Then she just sobbed.

Jackie's mother felt awful. She probably felt worse than Jackie. But what could she do?

We find it *very* hard to deal with our children's real sadnesses. It can tear us apart. Yet it is here that we have a very important role and we can be genuinely useful to our children. But only if we are not overwhelmed by their hurt.

"But I just feel so badly for her."

The first step for us in helping with the genuine hurts that our children experience is a very private one. We must deal with their hurts on *our* own, apart from them. With each real hurt we must grieve and again accept that our children's lives are not going to be without some genuine pain, some true disappointment, not quite the totally perfect childhood that we had hoped for them. We must accept that we cannot completely shelter them from the hurts that the real world does sometimes inflict.

But if we do allow ourselves to grieve for their hurts and accept their lives as they are, we can help.

"Nobody likes me. I hate school. I hate Debbie Prokowski. Why does this always happen to me?"

As Jackie sobs, her mother just sits there. Maybe she holds Jackie. Maybe she says comforting nothings like "I know, I know." But what she actually does is let Jackie's pain flow into her. If Jackie's mother has already grieved, she can allow this to happen. She will not be overwhelmed by her daughter's sadness and she can accept it. She can simply be there with Jackie. If she has already grieved, Jackie's mother does not have to try to deflect Jackie's pain. She will not need to say things like:

"It's not such a big deal. You'll see. There will be other birthday parties."

"It's not so bad. It will probably be a stupid party."

"Oh, I hate that Debbie Prokowski. I don't know what her problem is."

Nor does she sob along with her daughter.

If Jackie's mother can just sit there letting Jackie be upset, letting Jackie's hurt flow into her, and doing nothing with it but accepting it, and not being too upset by it, Jackie will start to feel better and, gradually, another reality will set in.

"Mommy still loves me. *She's not so upset.* I'm still me. Nothing has really changed."

If parents can deal with their children's very real hurts and not be blown away by them, they can be a great help to their children. Their child's pain then undergoes a subtle transformation from being a tragedy that affects their whole lives to something not quite so terrible after all. It is still a hurt for now, but a smaller hurt and they know it will pass.

But ultimately we and they are separate people. And especially as children get older our suffering for their pain can become progressively less useful to them. It can even become a burden.

"I'd never tell Mom about it. I know how much it would upset her."

Ultimately, what they may want is understanding, not that we suffer along with them.

One time, my Nick was sick—I think he had a stomach virus. I remember being in his room with him, having done all I could to lessen his suffering, but still he was in serious discomfort, which he was at that moment telling me. I remember saying to him, "You know one good thing about your pain?"

"What?" said Nick.

"It's not me who's having it."

And Nick laughed.

It was a joke. Because you and I are—really—two separate people, we both know that I can't do a thing for your pain. Zero. Which the baby self does not want to hear. But the mature self likes. It reaffirms its—Nick's own personal—dignity.

You *can* handle it. On your own. Since the truth is that I cannot do a thing for you.

Sensitive Children

One evening, seven-year-old Dexter's family planned to go out to Benji's Soft-Serve for ice cream. Dexter was really looking forward to it. But the car wouldn't start and by the time it was fixed, it was far too late to go out. Dexter was heartbroken. He sobbed and sobbed.

"Why? Why? Why can't we? Why?" The tears streamed down his face and his sobbing would not let up.

His father hugged him, rocked him, talked to him, offered him substitute treats.

"How about a popsicle? We have popsicles in the freezer."

But Dexter was inconsolable. If anything, the sobbing increased. "Noo. I want to go to Benji's."

Finally, Dexter did calm down, but it took literally a full hour of his father's doing all he could think of before his son was consoled.

"Dexter gets so upset. Little things that don't seem to bother other children devastate him. He's very sensitive."

There is no question that some children by their innate temperament are more high-strung, more easily upset than others. But parents need to be *very* careful about their responses to their often-heartbroken children where the tragedy, in and of itself, is not a tragedy at all. Whether or not their child is truly more sensitive to hurt than others, parents do not want to feed that sensitivity. The initial grieving may have been genuine grief, but the unending tragedy switches over to the wants of the baby self.

Dexter got an awful lot of parental response and special attention because of his being upset over the canceled ice cream outing, which no one would consider a tragedy. The message that he received was that he is very sensitive and that he *needs* more solace to deal with normal hurts and disappointments. That his hurts, for the same real life wounds—because he is he—are greater than other people's. A bad message. For it can help create someone who truly believes that his suffering is greater and more important than the suffering of others, and he therefore needs more attention than other people.

What parents need to do with the hurts of their children is to respond appropriately, not so much to the visible degree of upset but to the—in their adult judgment—degree of real hurt.

I am going to give more sympathy to a child who had been looking forward all week to a trip to the amusement park that fell through at the last minute than to a child whose ice cream trip was canceled.

What should Dexter's father have done? He needed to be consoling and sympathetic, but only to a point. When the sobbing continued past what seemed appropriate for an aborted ice cream trip, and when consoling did not help, he needed to back off.

"But why? I want to go to Benji's." Dexter's father no longer comforts, no longer hugs, no longer tries to offer alternative solutions. In truth, he is no longer sympathetic. He is saying that a canceled ice cream trip is only worthy of a certain degree of grief, and past that, no, I am not sympathetic at all. More often than not the griever, if ignored, will become angry: proof positive that this is no tragedy but rather the baby self being as demanding as always.

Children Who Worry

When I was little, each night before going to bed I used to check my closet and my dresser drawers to make sure no robbers were hiding in them. I knew that robbers could not fit in my dresser drawers, but it made me feel better just to make sure anyway.

Worrying is a part of childhood. Big worries. Little worries. Real worries. Unreasonable worries.

"Mommy, are robbers going to come in my room?"
"Daddy, am I going to die?"
"I'm scared. I'm scared the house is going to burn down."
"I don't want to go over to Jennifer's house because the last time I broke a glass by accident, and I know her mother is going to be mad at me."

Worrying is an inevitable part of life. That children worry is both totally normal and actually good. Worrying and responsibility are inseparable. Worrying is the price for gradually becoming independent and for truly taking the responsibility for one's own life. It is the price of being alone. It is the cost of separating from our parents.

As parents, our role is to comfort:

"Don't worry, my darling, we will always be here to protect you."

Our role is to help them know the real from the not real:

"No, there are no such things as ghosts."

We are there to reassure them:

"No robbers are going to hide in your closet."

And above all, we need just to be there:

"Do you want to sit on my lap?"

With most worrying, this is all our children need. But as with most childhood problems, we want to reassure, comfort, be there—only to a point.

Excessive Worriers

"Mom."

"What is it, Chad?"

"You will be there in front of the school when it's time to pick me up, right?"

"You know I'm always there, Chad."

"But what if you get into an accident?"

"We already went over this. If you feel that you have waited too long, go back into the school and wait in the office."

"But what if the school is locked?"

"I've told you it won't be locked. Somebody always stays late in the office just to make sure that all the children are picked up."

"But what if by accident they locked the door to the school?"

"Chad, it's not going to happen. There is not going to be a problem."

"But how do you know there couldn't be? You always say anything can happen. What if you are in an accident and they accidentally locked the school door? What will I do then?"

"Chad, that is not a realistic worry."

"But what will I do? I'm serious, I have to know or else I'm going to worry about it all day. You know I will."

And probably again, as she had in the past, Chad's mother would futilely try to reassure her son that there really was nothing to worry about. And probably again as on most days, Chad would head off to school still not totally satisfied.

"He worries so much. Nothing we say seems really able to reassure him."

Any parent of a chronic worrier knows that reassurances do not seem to help. They never seem satisfied. They seem to always come up with counterarguments and new worries. It is almost as if they do not want to be reassured. Yet if we were to hook up our lie detector and ask, "Chad, do you really want to be reassured or is this just some kind of act?" he would answer, "No, I'm really scared. I'm really worried." And the lie detector would show that he was telling the truth. Worriers do genuinely suffer.

But another player is running the show—the baby self, of course. And what it wants is not to be reassured but to be reassured unendingly. Plus if it had its way, it would not have to go out and deal with the world at all.

"But if it really were true that if I went to school and something terrible was going to happen, then you wouldn't want me to go to school. Right? Then I would have to stay home with you. Right? And if there were always terrible things that were going to happen I would always have to stay home, forever. Right?"

The baby self is too smart to talk quite that openly. But that is its goal.

But because it is the baby self who is running the show, the best parental strategy is very definitely not to try too hard to reassure. For it will not work.

Hence past initial reassurance—whether it works or not—parents do best backing off. And in fact there is ultimately a much greater reassurance that they can offer anyway.

True reassurance lies not in reasons why, but in the fact that one's parents are not worried. The unspoken but true reassurance is this: If it were a matter of real concern, I would be worried, but it is not, so I am not.

In fact, with true worriers whose parents refuse to get caught up in the endless reassurances, the baby self, who is most displeased when not getting its way, is frustrated. And often the worrying changes to anger. The baby self hiding behind the worrying shows its true face.

"You will be there in front of school when it's time to pick me up. Right?"

"Yes, I will be there, Chad."

"But what if you get in an accident?"

"I won't get in an accident."

"But what if you do? It could happen."

"I don't know what to say to you, Chad. We went all over this."

"But what if the school door is locked?"

"I don't know what to tell you."

"But you have to tell me. The school door could get locked and I won't know what to do. I'm going to worry all day."

"I'm sorry that you'll worry, Chad."

"But you have to tell me something. You have to tell me what to do."

By that point, Chad's mother does best to say no more.

"But you have to tell me what to do."

The baby self is frothing at the mouth. But if most excessive worriers were dealt with in this manner, the worries would become fewer. It works that way.

Bad Experience in Early Childhood—Trauma

When something bad happens to children that is beyond their capacity to handle, they often experience *emotional trauma*. Trauma is emotional hurt that is too much, that can neither be defended against nor easily healed. Trauma is hurt such as physical abuse, sexual abuse, or the death of a loved one—hurt that leaves a scar. Traumas can be big, like savage beatings over the course of a childhood, or small, like the suddenly discovered corpse of one's beloved cat. Obviously the smaller the trauma, the less the problem, and the bigger the trauma, the more time over which it is sustained, the worse the problem.

Major traumatic experiences lay down a painful imprint of intense bad feeling inside a child that does not go away. Terrible memories or feelings that come up repeatedly are a regular source of great pain. All too often the bad feelings get acted out upon another person—the abused becoming the abuser. Or a personality can warp itself in order to detour around the place of pain because it's too awful to even acknowledge. The terrible memories get placed in a room of no entry, an area that is totally forbidden. Yet bad feelings leak out nonetheless. And victims are left to puzzle at the strange bad forces within themselves whose origin they do not understand.

Some but not all serious traumas can be healed by time. The death of a parent, especially where there remains a second and continuing parenting figure, can gradually become a sad and a never forgotten part of a childhood that is positive overall.

Even with victims of serious abuse, continued nurturing and good life experiences gradually dull the sharp edges of an intolerable past. But not always.

Fortunately, most bad experiences are not traumatic, only very unpleasant, and there is much unpleasantness that children can handle without permanent damage.

"You don't have Jeremy? I thought you took him with you into the shoe store?"

"I thought he was with you in the supermarket."

Whereupon Jeremy's parents rush back to the parking lot where they find the sobbing two-year-old who has totally panicked, having been left alone for five minutes in the car.

Such experiences are traumatic in the sense that they are extremely upsetting to a child. But are the imprints of such experiences indelible? Do they change a life? Almost certainly they do not. Far and away the major shaper of personality is overall life experience, not single events. Where children have an overall happy life and their bad experiences are neither too awful nor sustained over time, parents can feel confident that their children have indeed not been scarred for life.

Difficult Children

An apocryphal story.

A mother and her son are in a McDonald's. In a booth across from them is a woman with five children who range in age from one to six. The mother of the five children is looking quite harried.

The first mother speaks to her and offers a trade. She will take the five children if the mother of five will take her child. Overjoyed with her good fortune, the mother of five accepts the trade offer. The children then go home with their new mothers.

Four days later the first mother receives a frantic call from the mother of the five children. "I want my five back, your Jamie is too much."

This is a story that I have told to a number of parents who have a child considerably more difficult than most. They like the story, knowing its truth, and also knowing that only parents of a child similar to theirs will ever believe that it could be true.

Some children by their nature—through absolutely no fault of their parents—are significantly more difficult than others. Many of these children are now described as having ADHD —attention deficit hyperactivity disorder, a diagnostic category that first came into existence in 1980.

All of what has been discussed in this book applies also to more difficult children. It is just that it may not work as well. But with them it is all the more important that parents not get caught up in all of the baby-self-generated back talk, arguing, case pleading, etc. that their child may throw at them. More difficult children with their poorer controls have double baby selves. They argue harder and longer. Hence, unless parents want to guarantee that they will become emotionally worn down, they *have* to be more businesslike—avoiding long explanations, avoiding long speeches intended to teach (which such kids genuinely cannot follow anyway), avoiding long anythings. With such children, unless all interventions are fast, clear, and firm, both child and parent will drown.

And, as discussed in regard to interventions—but especially so with more difficult children—one must pick and choose. One may have to ignore feet on the couch, eating in the family room, slamming the screen door, but not jumping on the couch which already has weak springs.

But the above can mean different rules within one family.

"You don't ever yell at Reggie for kicking the car seat and you always yell at me. It's not fair."

Rules with children do not have to be the same.

"That's right. I don't yell at Reggie. But I am right now yelling at you. Do not kick the car seat!"

Last and most important, as the parent of a more difficult child, whatever one does, one does not want to forget one's primary role as nurturer. These children, regardless of how they behave, must know that they are loved, and that even with all their exasperating behavior, they are just as good as all other children.

I know I am a brat. And I wish I could act better. But I just don't seem to be able to stop myself from doing bad stuff. I'd like to be good. I would. I don't want to be bad. I just do a lot of bad stuff.

Such children are enormously gratified and relieved if the fact is understood by their parents that in their hearts they are good. For it is easy for parents and the children themselves to lose sight of this. If they do, this more than anything else leads to future trouble. Instead, we want them to know:

I am good. It's just that often I don't act that way.

And if parents of more difficult children can survive their child's childhood and somehow come through it while communicating that though their child was truly more difficult— no question about that—they were no less good, no less loved, they have done very well indeed.

8

The Awesome Task
of Parenting

Thirty-four-year-old Barbara confronts her mother:

"You know that I have been miserable my whole adult life?"

"Well, yes, dear. And it makes me very sad."

"You know that I have gone through three marriages, can't form a stable relationship, have made a mess of my own children, and have been unable to hold a steady job?"

"Well, yes, dear. Your problems have been a source of great pain for me."

"You know that I have been in psychotherapy the last six months?"

"Yes, dear. I was pleased and I hoped that it might be helpful to you."

"Well, me and Dr. Schnedinger have decided that it's your fault."

"Oh, dear!"

"And I am very mad at you. You never were able to give. Everything was on the surface. Everything had to be nice.

You didn't want a child, you wanted a dress-up doll. You needed to hold yourself together to cover up your depression from your empty marriage with Dad and your awful parents. And you ended up starving me. That's why I have been so needy my whole life and wreck every relationship I ever got into. And it's all your fault."

"Oh, dear! I did try though. I did do what I thought was best."

"You did what you wanted. You shouldn't have had a child."

"Oh, dear! Oh, dear! I'm not feeling very well. Uhh! I think it's my heart."

"Mother. Are you okay? Mother?"

It is every parent's nightmare.

Or perhaps a simpler story, but just as awful:

"You know how you decided to leave me back in second grade?"

"Yes?"

"Well, it was a mistake. It ruined my life."

Ultimately, we do our best. I am not sure that any more can be asked of us. Hindsight is very easy.

"How could I ever have let them keep Anton back in second grade?"

But often we forget how at that time, where we were, looking at what we saw then, it did seem to be the best thing to do. In retrospect, perhaps it wasn't.

"Why can't you be like Beverly's mommy? She plays with Beverly all the time."

Maybe I am really not as good a mother as Beverly's mother. Maybe my two really would have been better off if they had been her kids.

Who knows? Maybe they would have been better off raised by Beverly's mother. But maybe the answer is that our children are not other people's children. They are ours. For better or for worse, that is their fate. And we can only do our best. But the good news is that usually that is plenty good enough.

"I did *my* best and my Leonard is the chairman of the board at Zedco Corporation. Is your Jeffrey still at the Correctional Institute? I heard they are giving him weekend passes."

The other half of it, of course, is that what we do with our children is not the whole story. The task of parenting is *not* akin to a sculptor confronted with a shapeless lump of clay. Not at all.

"My two sons, Reggie and Ronnie, are two years apart and they are as different as night and day. Reggie is always so keyed up. Full of energy. Quick to react. Nothing gets by him that he doesn't have something to say. But Ronnie has always been just the opposite. Laid back. Easygoing. Nothing much seems to faze him. And don't try to tell me that it is because I raised them differently. They were that way from the day they were born."

As is increasingly being shown by researchers in child development, children are born with varying psychological characteristics. We do not fully shape our children. Much they seem to bring with them.

In truth, our children are much more seed than clay. As parents we can add our piece, put in the ingredients of parenting—love, attention, encouragement, setting limits, making demands—but we will not be able to shape them exactly as we wish. It simply does not work that way. What we as parents do is important, hugely important, but it is also limited. Beyond the sum total of our input—good or bad—remain forces that shape who they become and over which we have no control at all. They take their own form. We can only put in what we feel are the best ingredients for growth, and then hope.

Conclusion:

Having a Childhood

What do I want for my children? That they have a childhood. That so long as nobody gets hurt, there be a place that is theirs. In which they are always okay.

I may stop them. I may tell them how obnoxious they are being. At times I may even deposit them somewhere else. But I do no more. And if in my heart, even when I do not like what they are doing and clearly let them know, I also truly deeply believe that whatever it is that they are doing is okay —they will hear this too. They will hear that with me there is this place, their childhood—that I do want them to have —a place where they are never bad, a place that is always safe and worry-free. A place of absolute nurturing.

And children who have been given this place do not grow up to be wild or disrespectful or to take advantage of others. Just the opposite. They become people who can give, care about others, and make the world in which they live a better place for their being in it.

Conclusion: Having a Childhood

And if a parent truly believes that giving a child this place —a childhood—is what is best, it turns out that that belief is a great aid in child raising. That it can make child raising so much easier and so much more pleasant.

For if parents truly believe that all the obnoxious, bratty, selfish behavior that they get is really not a big deal, is baby-self behavior, and that they want to make a place for the baby self, then parents will feel much less of a need to respond to all of the nonsense that the baby self throws at them when it is not getting its way. Which of course eliminates much of the baby self's most obnoxious behavior, the sole aim of which is to get as much of parent response as possible.

If I can allow them a childhood, they will give me the joy of being a parent.